Personal and Professional Development

# ASSESSING YOUR CAREER: TIME FOR CHANGE?

## Ben Ball

*Director, Career Development Unit,*
*University of Sussex, UK*

BPS
BOOKS
Published by The British Psychological Society

First published in 1996 by BPS Books (The British Psychological Society),
St Andrews House, 48 Princess Road East, Leicester LE1 7DR, UK.

A catalogue record for this book is available from the British Library.

ISBN 1 85433 198 1

Typeset by Gem Graphics, Trenance, Mawgan Porth, Cornwall, UK
Printed in Great Britain by Biddles Ltd, Guildford, Surrey.

## OTHER TITLES IN THE SERIES

# ASSESSING YOUR CAREER: TIME FOR CHANGE?

## Ben Ball

# Personal and Professional Development

SERIES EDITORS:

Glynis M. Breakwell is Professor of Psychology and Head of the Psychology Department at the University of Surrey.

David Fontana is Reader in Educational Psychology at University of Wales College of Cardiff, and Professor Catedrático, University of Minho, Portugal.

The books in this series are designed to help readers use psychological insights, theories and methods to address issues which arise regularly in their own personal and professional lives and which affect how they manage their jobs and careers. Psychologists have a great deal to say about how to improve our work styles. The emphasis in this series is upon presenting psychology in a way which is easily understood and usable. We are committed to enabling our readers to use psychology, applying it for themselves to themselves.

The books adopt a highly practical approach. Readers are confronted with examples and exercises which require them to analyse their own situation and review carefully what they think, feel and do. Such analyses are necessary precursors in coming to an understanding of where and what changes are needed, or can reasonably be made.

These books do not reflect any single approach in psychology. The editors come from different branches of the discipline. They work together with the authors to ensure that each book provides a fair and comprehensive review of the psychology relevant to the issues discussed.

Each book deals with a clearly defined target and can stand alone. But combined they form an integrated and broad resource, making wide areas of psychological expertise more freely accessible.

# Contents

# DEDICATION

To Gordon, my father

# PREFACE

The key premise of this book is that as individuals we are able to take responsibility for our own career choices and decisions, but that in order to do this effectively we need to develop our ability to review and plan our career moves and to take greater control over our working futures. Admittedly, career choices may entail a degree of compromise. It would be unrealistic to expect that we all achieve our career ideal. However, the possession of a range of career planning skills should at least make us more able to take advantage of opportunities that present themselves and increase our confidence in putting our ideas into practice. One key skill concerns self-appraisal – the process of reflecting on and identifying our own needs, values and abilities. It's what Charles Handy refers to as 'a proper selfishness' – the process of understanding our own strengths and weaknesses, of learning from our previous work experience. It lies at the heart of the career planning – the process of being able to make the next career move, of making and implementing career change.

This book, like a number of other career planning texts, is largely concerned with the process of personal reflection and self-appraisal which is an essential ingredient of career planning. The questionnaires and learning exercises which follow are designed to help you undertake this process, clarify your career ideas and assist in their implementation. In its origins the book owes much to its predecessor, *Manage Your Own Career*, which had similar objectives and offered a practical self-appraisal framework for the reader.

So can it work? Can books such as these act as a stimulus for change? People often question whether books and distance learning materials can ever help in clarifying complex life issues such as career choice, change and development. In evidence I can offer one simple anecdote to demonstrate the potential impact of materials such as these. Whilst working on the text for *Manage Your Own Career*, I was asked by the book's editor at the BPS for a copy of all the questionnaires likely to be used in the text. She wanted to work through them herself to see if they worked effectively. When next I telephoned to talk to her, I was informed that she had left the BPS to work in a different career in another part of the country. The text of *Manage Your Own Career* had been, it seems, largely responsible for her departure!

# Chapter One

# *All Change at the Workplace*

*What is happening is that industrial society is doing its best to hide the fact that the amount of socially necessary labour is declining rapidly and that everyone could benefit from this. Instead of proposing more free time for all those who want it, the only choice being offered is between full-time work or full-time unemployment – which is a way of presenting free time as a disaster, as social death.*

André Gorz, *Paths to Paradise: on the liberation from work*

Paid work, it seems, is an increasingly scarce commodity and the above quotation seems to represent a plea for a more even distribution of work and paid employment so that more people enjoy an equitable share of the work available. While the aim of this present chapter is not to rehearse the arguments for work sharing and/or a more even distribution of other employment, one particular theme underscores much of the change we are witnessing in the workplace, that of the tension between the aspirations of those in work or seeking work and the employment opportunities available to them. Exacerbated by recession, there are various points of tension: the increase in the numbers of long-term unemployed and the absence of available employment; the widening skills gap between the needs of business organizations and the skills offered by potential employees; the lack of career progression for those already in work; the diminishing sense of continuity and security experienced by many in the workplace, coupled with the gradual erosion of employee rights and benefits and the creation of a more 'casualized' workforce. All are to be found in the current workplace. And if the problems of unemployment and underemployment were not enough, we are faced with another characteristic of the workplace – change. Profound changes continue to take place in the nature of employment, the shape of business organizations, the manpower needs of the economy and in the opportunities available. In view of this rapid change the task for those making career choices and decisions is to understand something of the nature of the change we are experiencing, because this is the context in which our working lives are being enacted. The aim of this chapter is, therefore, to review the nature of the changes taking place in the workplace and to review the implications for us all. For those in demand, perhaps the highly qualified with much sought-after technical expertise, the concerns raised here may seem overstated, but few of us will be untouched by many of the features of working life in the 1980s and 1990s. And if there is one thing to be guaranteed, it is that change at work is not a temporary phenomenon. Change is a permanent state.

Three factors which have in particular exercised a major impact on the number and nature of the work opportunities available to us – the changing shape of business organizations, the continued shift in employment from one employment sector to another and the introduction of new technologies, particularly in formation technology – are summarized below.

# THE CHANGING SHAPE OF ORGANIZATIONS

A number of forces are thought to have changed the nature of business organizations and hence the jobs within them. Firstly, in the face of increased competition many companies have sought to reduce overhead costs by taking out entire tiers in their management structure, making them 'flatter' in organizational terms, thereby reducing the range of career ladders available to employees and, needless to say, making staff redundant. Commonly known as 'downsizing' or 'delayering', the process has typified much of the organization change of the early 1990s. Secondly, and more pervasively, managers have attempted to make organizations more flexible by employing a core of full-time permanent employees and a peripheral workforce of part-time, temporary and self-employed labour. 'Outsourcing' has become another management buzz word which has had major consequences for those at work, particularly in relation to employee benefits. It is a policy adopted by employers large and small alike. One result is that publishers, for example, no longer employ their own graphic designers; insurance companies no longer employ their own catering staff; even computing functions are now being 'outsourced', relying on freelance labour or contracted services rather than employing permanent staff.

A study of management careers in Britain, completed in 1993 by Inkson and Coe, provides evidence of the impact of 'delayering' and 'downsizing'. Among other findings, it emerged from a sample of Institute of Management members and their job changes over the previous 13 years, that managers:

- were being increasingly subjected to forced job moves as a result of changes imposed by their employers

- experienced fewer upward career moves and more lateral or downward moves

- made job changes more frequently despite the reduced options for personal and career development.

Although the authors acknowledge the effects of the recession in their findings, they none the less concluded that 'future career scenarios will be very different from the "onward and upward" view. In 1992, for example, the job changes experienced by managers were as likely to be reactive and determined by organisational pressures as they were proactive changes on the part of the individual managers'.

## EMPLOYMENT TRENDS AND OCCUPATIONAL CHANGE

Despite the problems of predicting the future nature of the world of work, there are nevertheless a number of broad trends that are taking place which look set to characterize the job market of the future, giving an indication of changes in the size of occupational groups and in work styles. The following summary is designed to provide a simple analysis of the changes that have already taken place and which look set to continue, based on projections by the Institute for Employment Research.

- Job growth will occur in management and in the professions, in health and personal services and sales, and among science and engineering professionals. Jobs in engineering trades, in unskilled factory work and in agriculture will continue to decline, continuing the shift from manual employment to 'higher level' occupations.

* In both the production sector and service sector, small firms create jobs. In the service sector in the late 1980s, small firms of less than ten employees accounted for half of net job creation.

* An increasing proportion of jobs will be part-time. In the 1980s over 1 million new jobs were part-time, and full-time jobs fell in number. A quarter of the entire workforce is now working part-time.

* As a consequence, female employment is rising faster than male employment, with the number of men employed actually falling in the decade to 1993.

* Jobs will continue to be lost in the manufacturing sector, with job growth concentrated in the service sector.

* Long-term unemployment is mainly concentrated among men. Few would wish to predict the future level of unemployment.

* Self-employment and home-working look set to increase further.

While stated very broadly, and not specific to any particular occupational group or business sector, the trends outlined above can provide the context in which career choices and decisions will be made. They support notions advanced by Stonier (1983) and Handy (1984) that the work of the future is going to be largely knowledge and information based – and hence demand a continuous 'upskilling' of the workforce. Many of the other implications for individuals at work are discussed below.

## CHANGING TECHNOLOGIES

The debate about the precise nature of the impact of technology on jobs and employment is an ongoing one. Pessimists point to the job losses arising from the introduction of new technologies. More optimistic observers point to the potential of technology to create jobs. In a detailed study of the impact of new technology in the workplace in the 1980s, Daniel (1987) concluded that technical change had a small part to play in the reduction in the number of available jobs, but raised the question of how far employers were able to avoid new recruitment and taking on additional staff as a result of the introduction of advanced technology. He also concluded that, on balance, new technology had the power to enrich jobs by increasing the level of skill and responsibility needed to carry out the work effectively.

In a more recent analysis, Freeman and Soete (1994) point to the potential of information and communication technology (ICT) both to change and destroy jobs as well as create them. On the one hand, they argue, the very pervasiveness of communications technology and its ability to process and transmit large quantities of information has brought about the changes in organizational structures referred to earlier, with the inevitable consequences for career development and jobs:

> *The world-wide intensification of competition based on rapid technical and organisational changes is leading to some dramatic changes in industrial structure as well as in management structure within firms. Large firms with rather top-heavy departmental and hierarchical structures faced particular difficulties. Because of rapid, easy access to information at all levels both vertically and horizontally, intermediate layers of management were often no longer necessary. The need for rapid response and greater decentralisation of responsibility within the new production and management systems also intensified this pressure towards 'downsizing' by reducing the number of middle managers.*

On the other hand, they point to the growth in jobs in computer software, which they suggest has been 'one of the fastest growing categories for new employment in the past decade'.

Whatever the precise effect of technological change on employment, we can be sure that it is having an increasing impact on the work style of individuals, on the development of service sector employment and hence on the kinds of jobs being created, as well as on the skills required of individual workers. It will also have an impact on job content. For which jobs have not been touched by information technology in one way or another?

## THE HUMAN IMPLICATIONS

Faced with the array of changes happening in the workplace, individuals have had to employ a range of coping strategies in order to survive effectively. Moreover, while the change in the nature of the labour market, in employment practices and in organizational needs has been well documented, the human cost has received far less attention. What have been the implications for individuals at work? What kind of impact has work change brought to their lives? What follows is a summary of some of these implications and an appraisal of the consequences for the career development of those concerned – a pointer to the psychological adjustment individuals have had to make to their notion of career and expectations of work and lifestyle.

## FORCED CHANGE

One outcome for many people has been that career change and job change has been a forced, not a voluntary, activity. The catering manager, redundant because her employer has contracted-out its catering services; the IT manager, redundant because his employer adopts a new computer system; the civil servant, edged into early retirement because of changes in public expenditure priorities; all provide examples of forced change. They do not include the vast number of individuals who have lost jobs and businesses because of downturns in the business cycle, because of recession and retrenchment. We all know of people who have been forced into a change of career direction, an altered course, for the reasons outlined above.

For many, this is a damaging and disabling experience, for some an opportunity for creative career change with wholly positive outcomes. The risk associated with forced change of this kind is that it makes the individuals concerned doubt their personal autonomy and ability to control their own future career development. It can reinforce an exterior locus of control, prompting individuals to assume that the job market either offers or denies opportunities and that they have little personal control over life events. The impetus for change of this kind can, of course, come from many different directions. In private companies the rationale used for organizational changes is not only that they have to keep pace with technological innovations, but also that in the face of international business competition they have to reduce their costs; or that faced with a merger or takeover, some elements of the business are no longer profitable. The net result is often the same – people lose their jobs.

Very often the changes enforced are seen to be at the whim of senior management and to have little justification. As one departmental manager in financial services put it: 'For years I've worked to make my department profitable and to keep a stable team of staff. I put a high store by maintaining people's commitment. Now I'm told that all this is wrong and that we must have change for its own sake. I've seen the management tier above me disappear and soon it will be my turn.'

In the public sector the impetus is often political. Public services need to be efficient and the government assumes that in order for this to be achieved services have to compete for the scarce financial resources available to them. The spirit of competition, however, does not rest easily with public sector workers whose personal aims have motivated them to work for the community good rather than compete with and out-perform colleagues doing similar work.

## AN UNCERTAIN FUTURE

While some of the trends in the job market are easily observable and one can make general assumptions about the kinds of jobs that are disappearing and those that are growing in number, there are few certainties for those starting or changing career. Most pundits and writers about job futures agree in predicting one thing – the future will be unlike the past. Change is a permanent state, whether it be in the nature of organizations, technologies or work styles.

For those of us thinking about our career development, there is considerable uncertainty about the future. Is it worth investing heavily in education and training for one particular career? Can those in mid-career who wish to retrain be sure that they won't meet with age discrimination when they look for work? Is it better to be a flexible generalist or a specialist in one particular field? These are the kinds of questions being faced by those reviewing their career options, and there are few certain answers.

An unpredictable and uncertain future may create a general feeling of insecurity, and for those wrestling with their career planning this raises considerable problems. On the one hand, there is little conventional wisdom to be passed from one generation to another about the nature of the opportunities on offer in the job market. Parents will have extreme difficulty in guiding their off-spring, because the nature of work has changed so rapidly, and previously held assumptions are no longer valid. The young have increasingly to envision their own working futures rather than accept conventional stereotypes. On the other hand, the process of deciding about career options has become more attenuated and more complex. In the absence of firm evidence about the nature of career paths and the long-term future of different occupations, those wanting to adopt a planned approach to their career have a considerable task in researching and evaluating the likely outcomes of different career options. As one public sector professional commented ruefully:

*The services we offer are at this time facing enormous change. We are effectively being privatised and the government is tilting the playing field, by encouraging absolutely anyone to become interested in managing us. It is very much politically motivated change, causing unnecessary work and insecurity, diverting our energies into setting up a limited company to bid for a contract to undertake our work against who knows what opposition.*

*My future career is therefore very unpredictable at present. I do not like imposed, unnecessary and unfair change. I am too young for early retirement, perhaps too old to go elsewhere, although my career has allowed me to develop a wide range of skills.*

Being able to cope with the strain of forced change is, it seems, one of the essential career maintenance skills for the 1990s.

## HIGHER DEMAND FOR QUALIFICATIONS AND SKILLS

Much more, it seems, is being asked of us in terms of qualifications and skills, with both employers and professional bodies raising their criteria for entry. This process is not a recent phenomenon, nor one that simply reflects a job market in recession. It reflects a longer-term trend that has been evident for some time.

It was Berg (1970) who pointed to the inexorable rise in the qualification levels being demanded of the American workforce, raising questions not only about the match of qualified people to the opportunities available, but also whether the highly qualified are always fully utilized in their work roles. Employers, he argued, are committed to raising entry qualification requirements because they see educational achievement as evidence of self-discipline, training potential and adaptability. Furthermore, the 'purposeless credential consciousness' was damaging to the education system in its promotion of an overtly instrumental view of the education process, one that is responsible for the 'vocational placement' of individuals in the workplace.

Government ministers and employer groups in the UK have used a rhetoric similar to their counterparts in the United States, arguing that higher skill levels are required because of:

- the increasing technological complexity of the workplace

- the need to remain competitive in the face of international business competition

- the desire for greater flexibility on the part of employees

- hoped-for gains in productivity and achievement arising from a better qualified workforce,

and perhaps, surprisingly, to make good the scarce skills gap in particular industries and technologies. There is also the implicit assumption held by many employers that highly qualified applicants are also the best intellectually and therefore deserving of a place in their core workforce, because of their development potential.

It is difficult to assess how far this message has been accepted by new entrants to the job market and those engaging in early- or mid-career change. Certainly, students are staying longer in secondary and further education. Participation rates in higher education have also increased dramatically. One in three 18-year-olds now undertakes some form of higher education. Between the years 1983 and 1993, the number of those graduating rose by over 40 per cent. Between 1988 and 1993, the numbers of post-graduates from 'established' universities grew by 45 per cent. How far these increases reflect the lack of employment opportunities is, of course, a matter for debate. It is interesting to speculate whether the growth in higher education would have been quite so spectacular had there been a buoyant job market, with plentiful job opportunities for younger workers.

Whatever the cause, it seems clear that the qualification spiral continues unabated. Entrants to chartered accountancy were once typically educated to A Level standard, but now there is largely graduate entry to the profession. Who would have predicted 30 years ago that management trainees in retailing would need 'a 2:1 degree from a prestigious university, with high levels of personal skills'. A 'graduate' job once implied a certain level of status in the job market, perhaps involving professional or management training. Now, cynics argue, a 'graduate' job is any job a graduate will do.

What are the implications for those involved in career planning? Given the competition for the work available and the stated needs of employers, it seems clear that we are obliged to invest more of our own time and money in the processes of education and training if we are to survive in the job market of the future, even if the likely return is uncertain and unpredictable.

## WORKING HOURS, WORKING LIVES

The job market for young people all but collapsed in the early 1980s and is unlikely to reappear. Few 16–18-year-olds will now go directly into employment, but instead undertake vocational training or remain in education. At the same time, the participation of 18-year-olds in higher education is increasing. For example, between 1980 and 1990 the number of first-year students in higher education rose by 44 per cent, as more and more people opted for further and higher qualifications, and delayed their entry into the job market. How far this behaviour was motivated by the need to gain qualifications for an ever more competitive job market is open to question. What is clear, however, is that in future working life and regular paid employment will start later for many of those about to enter the job market. And while many students will have voluntary experience, or will have worked casually to finance themselves through their education, many will in effect delay their entry to a particular 'career'.

Faced with the problem of high unemployment and the need to share work, any rational economic system's solution would argue for a reduction in the time spent at work for every individual. In fact, just the reverse is happening; many people are working longer hours. I remember asking a group of public sector employees whether they had expected their working hours to decrease over their career span. They were unanimous in their reply. They had all expected to spend fewer hours at work as time progressed. When I asked them to compare their current working hours and leave entitlement with those ten years previously, the result was predictable. None had experienced a diminution in work time. Indeed, it is now clear that for some core workers, working hours actually increased, creating more problems for those trying to balance work and non-work, home life and workplace. A survey in 1993 by the Institute of Management revealed that three quarters of respondents had seen their workload increase in the previous year as organizations stripped out layers of management. Nearly 45 per cent disagreed with the statement 'I have a good balance between home and work'. 40 per cent of those surveyed worked at least 50 hours per week.

A parallel process is taking place for those reaching their career end. Perhaps for a variety of reasons – the incipient ageism of many employers, the increasing incidence of work stress, obsolescent skills – fewer and fewer employees are working until normal retirement age. Early retirement is increasingly a feature of many white-collar jobs, as many older employees are eased out of their jobs, with 'early release' enticements and pension deals. As one recruitment specialist in a major UK company put it, 'You have to be a very senior manager to work here after the age of 50'. The net effect of a later start to working life and an earlier end, together with, in some cases, increased working hours, is an intensification of work, a shorter opportunity to earn a financial return, and the need to achieve against a shorter time-scale.

## EMERGING WORK STYLES

If permanent full-time paid employment is rapidly diminishing, what is to replace it? According to Charles Handy (1993), a new work style is emerging in response to the changes mentioned earlier – less secure, more risky and entrepreneurial than a permanent job. Handy uses the term 'portfolio careers' to describe how different bits of work in our life can fit together to form a balance. The main ingredients of the portfolio are:

- wage work – money paid for time given

- fee work – money paid for results

- home work – unpaid work in the home, DIY, cleaning, etc.

- gift work – voluntary work

- study work – training or education, for example, learning a new language.

Whereas previously our working lives were dominated by wage work, particularly for men, Handy now sees the possibility of a newer form of working life – a mix, possibly, of part-time work and freelance working, offering greater flexibility for the work and potentially greater autonomy and control. The following case studies offer a glimpse of this future, but are based on real people and present day experience, rather than portraying an example of what might be at some stage in the future.

### ❏ Case Study: Helen
*Helen is an accountant and works for a firm of insolvency practitioners. She has an office at home and goes into the firm's office one day a week. When businesses go into voluntary liquidation, Helen interviews the*

*directors, draws up financial proposals which they can make with their creditors and which then form the basis of a court order. Helen has to travel a great deal, attends court and relies heavily on a network of contacts for business referrals.*

*She enjoys the work style, in particular being her own boss and organizing her own schedule of work which may involve evenings and weekends. This flexibility enables her to spend time with the children, and in general work fits in around family life rather than the reverse. If she wants to, she can work in the evenings, or whenever it suits. The disadvantages are common to many homeworkers. She doesn't feel part of a team and finds motivating herself difficult. On balance though, she would hate to go back to a normal office routine.*

*Although the job provides a basic salary, Helen's earnings also depend on commission based on the amount of work she generates. The workload is uncertain and unpredictable and so is her income.*

## ❑ Case Study: Clare

*Clare works on a freelance basis designing and monitoring clinical trials for new pharmaceutical products and reporting the results. She had previously worked for a major pharmaceutical company as a clinical research assistant and, therefore, had considerable experience of the work already. She admits she was unaware that freelancing was an option until she heard about it from a friend. Now her home is her work base and she has two short-term contracts lasting anything up to two years, part home-working, part based on the contractors' premises. Her early nursing experience helped with the setting up of the clinical trials in hospitals and health centres and provided her with background knowledge and a ready technical vocabulary.*

*Working freelance offers her variety and considerable psychological freedom. She plans her own workload, gives herself time for holidays when she likes and it has given her the chance to work voluntarily in Eastern Europe. There are, however, disadvantages. As sole breadwinner she finds herself having to live with financial uncertainty. Any period of ill-health causes particular problems. There is also the sense of isolation – not being part of a team and always an outsider. And what kind of person do you need to be to make a success? Firstly, you have to be good at budgeting and planning personal finances. In addition, you need to maintain your professional credibility and network effectively to maintain your work contacts.*

As the case studies illustrate, this kind of work style can have its disadvantages, in particular the uncertainty and lack of security associated with freelance working. In some people's eyes, it would also represent a rebuttal of the right to employment and to have a 'proper' job; a precarious work style which represents a second-best, a 'scratching around' for any work that is available. According to Handy, this is very symptomatic of yesterday's thinking and we should all prepare ourselves for a portfolio future. Certainly, neither of the individuals highlighted above actually wanted to return to permanent office-based employment, which shows how people value both autonomy and flexibility. In both cases, however, it is fair to point out that the 'portfolio' approach arrived by chance and in mid-career. It was not necessarily expected or planned for. It also depended on each individual having both contacts and the professional credibility to establish themselves in their particular specialism. This suggests that portfolio working may not always be possible for younger workers unless they have immediately employable skills which can be used for fee work. New entrants in the job market may therefore need to rely more heavily on paid employment in order to develop their profile of experience, before launching on a portfolio work style.

A freelance work style often implies an element of homeworking. Many more people are using the home as a work base, investing in a range of office equipment to enable them to communicate effectively and to produce their work, whether it be a magazine article, a design for a book jacket, accounts spreadsheet or a research report. Traditionally associated with hourly-paid, semi-skilled work, homeworking is now associated with a very different kind of activity, often of a professional or semi-professional nature. Freelance consultants, trainers, editors, all use the home as a work base, much in the way that university lecturers have done and still do.

Homeworking is, however, not the exclusive preserve of freelancers. A number of employed workers also work from home. Results from a survey by Huws (1994), revealed that one in ten employers uses some form of homeworking. Approximately half of these employ teleworkers, that is staff who work remotely from home using information technology. The staff concerned worked in a variety of ways: as permanent or temporary employees, as freelancers or sub-contractors, as pensioners on retainers or agency staff. There was no one single predominant work style. While there were benefits for employers in terms of reduced costs and space requirements, the main benefits to employees were twofold – the avoidance of commuting and having the flexibility to care for children by balancing work life and home life. The incidence of teleworking was found at a variety of occupational levels and in a wide range of different kinds of work. A common work style for translators, researchers, writers and editors, it was also used by computer professionals, those offering secretarial services, in financial services and accountancy, as well as various forms of consultancy. Many of the stereotypes applied to homeworking were apparently unfounded. Teleworkers were mainly, but not exclusively, women. The hours worked suggested that it was a full-time rather than a part-time activity. Many occupational groups spent at least some time on their employers' premises. This, of course, depends on whether the teleworker is deemed to be an employee as opposed to a freelancer.

Where staff had been selected to work at home by their employer, there was a clear implication that those without training were unlikely to be considered – 'only the most trusted, experienced and highly motivated staff were selected for telework.'

The 'home' view of teleworking as opposed to the employer view has been explored in some detail by Haddon and Silverstone (1995). The choice of teleworking as a work style, it seems, is sometimes involuntary, with women workers in particular adopting it as a way of combining work with child care. Even the reasons for adopting it on a voluntary basis were said to be in order to avoid a worse situation – as a reaction to work problems; to avoid long-distance commuting; as a reaction to possible redundancy. The authors caution against a simplistic view of the benefits of homeworking, concluding that 'no two male or female experiences of teleworking are identical'.

They also found that teleworking was not necessarily a permanent work style but 'a provisional, perhaps temporary commitment', particularly for women taking a career break from permanent employment. People embarked on teleworking from a variety of experiences: from part-time work, from full-time study, from full-time office-based employment. Some of those interviewed in the study, however, saw teleworking as a conscious lifestyle choice, entailing more of a permanent commitment.

If 'fee' work is increasing at the expense of wage work, what evidence have we about the incidence of self-employment and its benefits for the individuals concerned? Certainly, the numbers in self-employment have risen considerably, doubling in the 1980s, but questions remain about whether this way of working is adopted positively for the flexibility and autonomy it offers, or as a response to the problem of not being able to find paid employment. A study by Meager, Court and Moralee (1994) suggests that both factors may be operating. Incomes from self-employment were seen to vary more widely than those for paid employment – with a self-employed person having 'over three times the odds of being in the poorest tenth of the distribution of individual labour incomes than does an employee'. A picture therefore emerges of some high earners, with men over-represented in this group, and a group of 'poor' self-employed which is more likely to be comprised of young women workers in personal service occupations. The earning potential of the 'new' self-employed and their financial security, both immediate and long-term, will be a matter of concern for those considering this particular work style.

Indeed, there are those who argue that the 'new' self-employed experience the same lack of employment rights and benefits as temporary or seasonal workers, that they have problems in maintaining a continuity of earnings and, furthermore, that they have little of the bargaining power of those in salaried employment. As many freelancers will attest, securing an adequate pay rate for your work in line with increased inflation is a stiff task when so many contractors and freelancers are looking for work.

## CHANGING ASSUMPTIONS ABOUT 'CAREER' AND CAREER DEVELOPMENT

The changes referred to earlier in the way people are employed and the evolving nature of their employing organizations have forced us to rethink our notion of what is meant by the term 'career' and to acknowledge a new set of assumptions about our working futures.

The idea that individuals follow a stable straight-line career path to retirement with one employer has to be revised to acknowledge that many of us will experience one or more major changes of career in our lives and that career paths are going to be increasingly interrupted and diverted, creating less job security. For some, periods of employment will be interspersed with periods of unemployment. For others, work will comprise a number of different part-time jobs, various forms of contract work or periods of temporary work. For others still there will be the prospect of long-term unemployment, a jobless future. People will need in future to be prepared for a more interrupted career pattern, recognizing that a number of job and career changes may be necessary to give them the work satisfaction they need.

Going too, is the notion of 'career' as a sequence of 'better jobs'. For many people, the word 'career' implies a series of jobs, each one involving more responsibility or better pay; a pattern of upward mobility. The 'tea boy to managing director' story was never the reality for the majority of the working population and is now even more remote. The hierarchical nature of most organizations ensures that a few people reach the top, whilst the majority perform other, less well-paid work. Given the changing shape of organizations, the prospects for upward progression and promotion become even more remote. Flatter organizations offer fewer rungs on the promotion ladder. For many, career development will be a series of sideways moves – going to a different company, but doing the same job; moving to a different, but similar status job within the same company. For others, there will be apparently downward moves. The fifty-year-old redundant executive may have difficulty in finding a job of similar status and be prepared to settle for something less demanding, or more likely, opt for freelance or portfolio working.

It is paradoxical, of course, that this should be happening at a time when employers are beginning to recognize that, in an information society, it is the organization's human resource which is the most crucial for long-term survival, rather than particular products or industrial processes. And when their value is apparently recognized as never before, organizational commitment to employee career development is becoming weaker. With such rapid change taking place, employing organizations can also appear to be giving contradictory messages to their employees and potential job seekers, as different groups of workers acquire more importance than others. At the very time that organizations are involved in large-scale redundancy programmes which affect clerical or manual workers, they can also be recruiting new graduates or key professional workers for their 'core' activities. The rhetoric of employers and employer groups often appears to fly in the face of everyday realities.

There is also a growing acknowledgement that the term 'career' is no longer simply equated with paid employment. For those in freelance or part-time work, perhaps working as contractors for a range of different organizations, career development may be concerned with balancing a variety of roles and work demands. For women, particularly, who interrupt employment for family reasons, 'career' will be concerned with childrearing, part-time paid work and, possibly, voluntary work. Career development will take in family, personal and community roles. A 'career break' will increasingly be a time for continued professional updating by distance learning. The re-entry to employment will be characterized by flexible hours and/or job share schemes.

For those leaving higher education, also, there is a growing acceptance that voluntary or part-time work experience may be an essential way of gaining entry to particular career paths. Would-be social workers and clinical psychologists need a range of relevant experience prior to professional training – voluntary work is viewed as being as important as paid employment in providing this essential experience.

The notion of a 'stage' or 'internship' providing short-term work experience provides a further example of the way skills and experience can be enhanced, without a commitment to permanent paid employment.

Finally, there is the realization that employers cannot commit themselves to the career management of individual employees, at least not in European countries. Japanese companies may endorse a 'cradle to grave' commitment to their employees, but most western employing organizations are generally unwilling to provide this kind of commitment. It is true that in some large organizations there has been an attempt to manage the progression of particular staff up the organizational ladder. It happens particularly in the case of fast-track management training schemes, but these are in the minority. Most employees have to demonstrate their potential for promotion rather than expect their career progression to be a managed process, with well defined stages. For most people, career progression, if it exists, is characterized by unpredictability and happenstance. A full analysis of the ways organizations can help employees in their personal and career development is presented later.

The new assumptions about career development are summarized in the following box. There are others, of course. Retirement, so often in the past seen as 'being put out to grass', is now, with the lowering of the effective retirement age and increased longevity, seen as the Third Age, in which people continue their development, both personal and career.

---

CHANGING ASSUMPTIONS ABOUT WORK

| **Traditional Assumption** | **Emerging Assumption** |
| --- | --- |
| Full employment is sustainable. | Full employment is not likely to return in the foreseeable future. |
| Most people follow a stable, straight-line career path to retirement. | Career paths are increasingly going to be diverted and interrupted. |
| Career development means upward mobility. | Career development can be facilitated by lateral and downward moves. |
| Only new or young employees can be developed. | Learning and change can occur at any age and career stage. |
| Career development relates primarily to work experience and can take place only in one's job. | Career development is influenced by family, personal and community roles, and can be facilitated by work outside paid employment. |

---

## TAKING CHARGE OF YOUR OWN CAREER

These revised assumptions have particular implications for those of us making career choices and changes. Firstly, we need the flexibility to be able to adjust to change: occupational change and technological change. There is little that appears to be predictable about the workplace of the future.

Secondly, in order to cope with job and career change, we need to equip ourselves with a range of skills which will help us manage our careers, because employing organizations are not going to do it for us. Among those skills are the ability to review our experience and appraise our own skills and potential, to research opportunities in the workplace and make a match or synthesis of the two. Finally, we need to have a plan of action to help us achieve our goals.

Being able to anticipate job and organizational change, to engage in networking across organizational boundaries, to cope with unexpected and unanticipated change, are also some of the skills involved. But alongside these we need to acknowledge the importance of those concerned with effective self-presentation and job search, to be able to maintain our self-esteem in the face of rejection or the lingering threat of redundancy.

In short, the more proactive the behaviour we can engage in, the more likely it is that we will find work activities which satisfy our needs. And, as recent research has shown, the more 'decided' we can be about our overall career direction, the more likely we are to be successful in our search for work. The following chapters will illustrate how, in practice, you might take greater control over your career and help you to give your career the attention it deserves.

# Chapter Two

# *Choosing and Changing*

*No year will seem again quite so ominous as the one when formal education ends and the moment arrives to find employment and bear responsibility for the whole future. I was hemmed in by a choice of jails in which to serve my life imprisonment, for how else at twenty can one regard a career which may last as long as life itself, or at the best until that sad moment is reached when the prisoner is released, in consideration of good behaviour, with a pension?*

Graham Greene, *Fragments of an Autobiography*

One can infer a lot of things from Graham Greene's account. Firstly, that he was afraid of making a major commitment to one particular career; secondly that he was rather hoping that someone else might suggest what he might do with his life; and thirdly, that he viewed working life as a form of prison sentence! For some people – the lucky few – career choice can be a relatively simple process. For many of us, however, career decisions are complex, bringing into play a range of factors: our aspirations, our sense of self, in particular our own constructs and personal values.

Greene's account highlights a number of common perceptions that people hold about career choice and decision-making which are sometimes problem-creating and often self-limiting. It is important to look at these in some detail, because they both hinder our ability to make changes on our own behalf and do nothing to enhance our feelings of self-esteem.

# SELF-LIMITING BELIEFS

What follows is a summary of the more commonly held perceptions which may need to be challenged if we are to develop our careers successfully.

You may identify with one or more of them. If you do, it will be useful to discuss them further with a partner, colleague or mentor. There may be other perceptions, conscious or unconscious, that are holding you back from taking action to choose or change a career.

## CAREER CHOICE IS IRREVERSIBLE

The thought that it is difficult to change career direction may serve only to heighten the perceived importance of the decision with which you are faced. For those like Graham Greene, who are just about to graduate from higher education, career choice takes on the appearance of a major life decision, which many graduates would really rather avoid. It is also particularly acute for those in mid-career who have undertaken full-time study or training. They feel that for them time is limited. They have little opportunity to experiment and, because they have often made a big financial investment in their education or training programme, they may feel considerable pressure to make the 'right' decision about their future career direction. For other people, the process of making a career decision is hampered by a fear of commitment. To accept one career option is to reject all others, which can result in a sense of wanting to keep as many options as possible open, rather than focus on one or two in particular.

In practice, of course, career change is not only possible, but increasingly likely, given the scenario outlined in the first chapter. Tomorrow's job market demands change and those who are more adaptable or flexible in their approach to career development are likely to feel more in control of their lives.

## THERE IS A SINGLE 'RIGHT' CAREER FOR EVERYONE

This perception is often closely allied to the one above. People may believe that their ideal job exists somewhere in the job market and that their task is to find out where it is. The talent-matching theories of career development, described below, sometimes serve to support this belief. In fact, of course, we are multipotential and can turn our hand to a number of different jobs. We are motivated in our career development, however, to ensure that our work meets, progressively, our needs and values and provides an outlet for our individual skills and interests, while at the same time our aspirations are mediated by our experience and personal circumstances.

## EVERYBODY ELSE SEEMS TO KNOW WHAT TO DO

We have difficulty accepting that to be confused and undecided is a perfectly normal and natural state and that our experience is being shared by those around us. Sometimes, of course, individuals have no doubts about their future career direction – jockey Lester Piggott described how at the age of four he knew that his future would be concerned with horses and racing. These are, however, the exceptions.

### 'IF I TAKE TIME OUT OR DISTANCE MYSELF FROM THE SITUATION I MIGHT FIND THAT A CAREER DECISION WILL COME TO ME'

One of the more common responses of new graduates when faced with the decision about a 'career' is to take time out to travel the world in the hope that somewhere, perhaps in the Hindu Kush, a form of divine inspiration will provide them with the answer to the big question 'What am I going to do with the rest of my life?' Sadly, most return with the question still unanswered, albeit with some revised perspectives on life and its meaning.

Planned procrastination is, of course, another thing. A conscious decision to postpone the process of career choice is understandable, but the hope that life experience will by itself provide a career strategy is likely to prove a vain one and not deliver an immediate result.

For many, therefore, 'taking time out' can be more a question of decision avoidance than a planned exercise in personal development.

## IT'S ALL A QUESTION OF LUCK

In a short story called *Lucky Break*, Roald Dahl describes how, in wartime United States, the writer C. S. Forester asked him to provide some notes about his front line experiences which could be used by Forester for an article for the *Saturday Evening Post*. Dahl duly obliged, but seized the opportunity to present a finished piece about his wartime exploits. In the event Forester arranged for the piece to be printed in full under Dahl's name, describing it as the work of a gifted writer.

You could accept, of course, that this was a lucky break for Dahl, but equally you could argue that he created the opportunity by working through the night to produce a highly polished piece of writing. In career planning most of us have to create our own luck in the same way. A belief that life events are necessarily shaped by luck and chance is, of course, highly dysfunctional for the career changer, and the career planning model which follows is designed as an antidote to this way of thinking. Luck may play a part in the opportunities that present themselves, but we have to develop the ability to recognize and sense an opportunity when it occurs.

### 'THERE MUST BE AN EXPERT SOMEWHERE WHO CAN TELL ME WHAT I'M SUITED FOR'

It's tempting to believe that somewhere there is an expert who can make an assessment of the kind of work you would be ideally suited for. One career changer described how she wished she had been living in a communist state, so that she could have been allocated a job rather than make the decision herself. Careers psychologists may be able to assess your personality and abilities and suggest occupations for which you might be suited but few would want to predict what might be your ideal job. The truth is, we are multipotential, capable of a wide variety of different kinds of work.

Other beliefs are commonplace. 'I can't do it, because I've no relevant experience.' 'There are five hundred applications for every job, so there's no point in my applying.'

Many of these 'problematic' generalizations and self-observations have a limiting effect on career development. Many result from low self-esteem and lack of confidence. Others, plainly, enable individuals to erect imaginary barriers to career goals and close off avenues for change and growth rather than explore them further. They also accompany feelings of inertia and a reluctance to take action. As one undecided graduate put it, 'I was getting to the stage where I was waiting for something to happen and, of course, it never did.' While many of the examples quoted above are commonly made by those making initial career choices, they are also shared by potential career changers. 'No-one's going to want me at my age.' 'There's no point in going for promotion, I'm not experienced enough.' are the kinds of self-limiting beliefs voiced by would-be career changers.

One of the tasks, therefore, for both career choosers and changers is to keep an open mind rather than impose limits on one's career development based on untested assumptions – a theme to which we will return in later chapters.

## WHAT FACTORS INFLUENCE CAREER CHOICE AND DEVELOPMENT?

One of the main aims of this book is to encourage you to take an active approach to resolving career choices and decisions and to do so in the most effective way. The exercises which follow in the next chapter were designed with this in mind. As a precursor, it might be helpful to review some of the theory of career decisions – why individuals choose one particular career rather than another, how career needs vary over a lifespan and what motivates people in their work.

There is a large body of psychological research concerned with the process of occupational choice and development. Several different theories attempt to explain why individuals choose one kind of work rather than another, each with a different emphasis. They are in essence complementary, each with a particular contribution to make to the main question. You may be able to espouse the claims of one rather than another theorist by reflecting on your own experience in making choices and decisions.

### INDIVIDUAL DIFFERENCES

It seems mere common sense to suggest that people are different and as a result will tend to take up different occupations. And this view, derived from early twentieth century studies of individual differences in terms of ability and personality, is one that still forms the basis of most current practice in career guidance. Satisfactory career choice accordingly is achieved by obtaining a satisfactory match between the traits of individual job seekers and the demands of different jobs. It's easy to see why the emergence of this 'talent matching' perspective on entry to the workplace so clearly reflected the processes of industrialization of the early twentieth century and the need to make effective use of the labour force.

Of all the theories exploring the nature of individual differences in career choice and development, those concerning personality differences have attracted considerable research interest. According to John Holland (1966) one's choice of occupation is an expression of personality, and his work is based on the assumption that people can be classified into six basic personality types: realistic, investigative, artistic, social, enterprising and conventional, and in making career choices people search for work environments which correspond to or provide an outlet for the expression of their personality type.

| Personality type | Personal characteristics |
|---|---|
| Realistic | Has mechanical abilities, is practical and materialistic. |
| Investigative | Has mathematical and scientific interests. Is analytical, rational and reserved. |
| Artistic | Expressive, intuitive, independent types who exhibit creativity. |
| Social | Likes to inform, train or develop people. Good communicator. |
| Enterprising | Likes persuading, exercises leadership. Seen as ambitious, energetic and opportunistic. |
| Conventional | Prefers systematizing data, careful and orderly. |

In order to assess individuals according to their particular type, Holland developed the Self Directed Search, a questionnaire designed to elicit the three most highly scored 'types', arguing that for consistence individuals were likely to have a profile score relating to three of the types which were related. For example, according to Holland it would be consistent to have high scores for Realistic, Conventional and Investigative (RCI) but not Realistic, Artistic and Conventional (RAC). In reviewing the different descriptions you may be able to say which three types seem to fit your own personality.

One appeal of Holland's work is its usefulness in classifying occupations and generating career ideas which fit the various personal styles. It's easy to see, for example, that Realistics might prefer technician jobs in engineering, Conventionals in finance and Socials in teaching, social work or applied psychology! As a result, the RAISEC model forms the basis of a number of computer-assisted guidance systems as well as distance learning personal and career development materials.

Another set of explanations of career choice and development is derived from studies of life-span development. According to Donald Super (1981) career decisions are not a single event in time, but rather part of a developmental process evolving over time, with individuals using their job or career as an expression of their self-concept, their ideas of themselves, which comprise their abilities, values, needs and personality. Super suggested that we move through five accelerated stages of career development: growth, exploration, establishment, maintenance and decline and that these stages mediate the career decisions we make, as do other life events and concerns. Typically, fantasy choices give way to tentative approaches to career, followed eventually by a more established stage, and so on. A key emphasis in Super's work is that the way individuals conceive of themselves and the world of work influences their career choices and decisions.

This is supported by several research studies which show that those with low self-perceived competence are more likely to have restricted occupational choices. This may account for the career behaviour of women who often have, according to research findings, lower self-efficacy expectations than their male counterparts.

A further dimension to the developmental perspective on careers is provided by Levinson (1978) whose study of individual life histories suggests that individuals characteristically encounter a number of major life transitions which are age-related. Negotiating these life stages frequently involves people in a review of career and life goals and is therefore significant in career development terms. The age 30 transition and the 'mid-life crisis' are, according to Levinson, both critical events in the life span which may trigger a major life change.

Other theories of career choice stress the importance of the cognitive process involved in combining the knowledge of ourselves with knowledge of occupations. Accordingly, we need to understand the thought processes which underpin the process of career decisions if we are to make the process more effective. If we use irrational beliefs or engage in negative self-perceptions, this will have an impact on our career behaviour. Another branch of career theory stresses the importance of learning experiences which may influence both our views of particular occupations and the evaluations we make of ourselves. If, for example, we have positive experiences of particular subjects in secondary or higher education it is more likely that we will seek occupations which build on or relate to the subjects we have studied.

The career planning approach which forms the basis of this book acknowledges and makes use of a wide range of different career theories and is not espoused to any one particular theoretical model. Understanding the different perspectives should help you in the process of choosing, changing or developing your career and will certainly enable you to test your own ideas about future stages in your career development.

## MAKING YOUR OWN CAREER DECISIONS

You may want to espouse one theory or another. Certainly a range of factors influence people's career choices and decisions, and this and the following chapter attempt to explore some of these in more detail.

Whatever the explanations for people's choices, most career changers and job seekers simply need a model which is going to help them towards a personal choice – a way of deciding what to do. They need answers to some basic yet important questions – What options are available to me? What am I capable of? How do I go about deciding what to do? The method outlined below is called career planning (see Figure 2.1) and if followed systematically can take you through the process of choosing a career path. Perhaps a word of definition is required here, however. 'Career planning' describes the range of activities used by individuals to determine their next career move. The process normally includes a personal review of experience, skills and values, defining career objectives and finding ways of implementing ideas of change and development. It is not equivalent to charting a life-long path through working life or attempting to predict where you might be at any particular time. We can seldom predict life events with that degree of accuracy. Rather, it is a continual process of review, to be engaged in on a regular basis, to facilitate the career decision process. Furthermore, you can use it at any stage in your life to decide on your next step. It is as applicable at the age of 51 as it is at the age of 21, for both mid-career change and initial choices. Once learned, the method can be used at any stage in one's career development.

## STAGES IN CAREER PLANNING

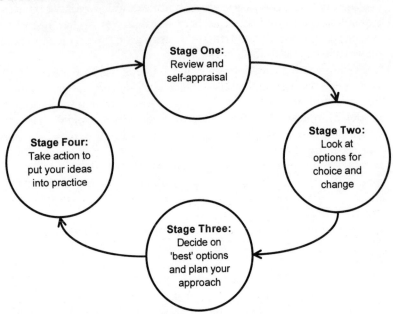

*Figure 2.1:* Stages in Career Planning

Not everyone will want to follow a logical sequence in thinking about career choice or change, preferring to let chance take a hand or take any option which seems readily available, rather than look for work which is intrinsically interesting. Alternatively, they may not want to take a planned approach. They may want to act spontaneously and simply respond to a need for variety and change. As one career changer put it,

> *My own career changes have never been planned as such. They have often arisen from my own perceptions of personal inertia, a need to move to a fresh challenge.*

For those who want to take the issue of career development systematically, however, there are, when making a career move, a number of stages that are important to work through and which build on one another. Your precise starting point is not a vital consideration; it is a cyclical process. You can start at Stage Two and work back to Stage One, for example, but it may help if you start at the beginning. The series of questionnaires presented in the next chapter are intended to take you through Stage One, that of compiling a career and personal development profile. Later chapters in the book are designed to prompt you in your subsequent decisions and action plans.

## WHAT ARE THE ADVANTAGES OF A CAREER PLANNING APPROACH?

Most job seekers and career changers will intuitively follow the stages outlined above and because it may seem like applied common sense, you may wonder why it needs to be made so obvious. In fact, done properly, career planning is a skill that, once learned, can be applied again and again at different stages in your life, and like most skills, is capable of the further refinement which comes from continued practice and rehearsal. What's more, working through the process will bring you a range of added benefits.

A career planning approach can:

- *put you in charge of your own future.* There is often a big temptation to abdicate responsibility for life decisions to other people. After all, isn't that what career advisers are for? Or parents? Or partners? The truth is, no matter how difficult it may be to achieve, your future lies in your hands.

- *help you to feel more positive about yourself and your future.* Setting a goal for the future and writing down a plan of action can, for most of us, be tremendously energizing. Behaving proactively can also bring an increase in self-confidence. Instead of spending time agonizing about a decision, you will feel more in control for having taken action, even if your initial steps meet with only limited success.

- *be a creative process.* You may have entertained ideas for your future for some time but perhaps not acknowledged their significance, described them to others or even written them down. Career planning can encourage you to open your mind to the range of possibilities that might be available to you, and you may well find there are more than you think. In addition, career planning can help you define areas of work and jobs that don't exist now but which will do in the future.

- *embrace a range of personal and life goals.* There is no reason why you should limit your future goals to the relatively narrow question of 'What job to do next?' Career planning involves setting goals for personal and career development, for work and life as a whole. In fact, it goes under many headings such as 'life/work planning', 'career management', etc. In any case, a new career path will almost certainly involve you in further study, training or other development activity.

- *improve your chances of success.* In making your applications succeed, you will need to show your commitment to a particular career goal. Recruiters simply can't entertain the 'I'll do whatever job you have' approach from applicants. In addition your CV or application letter will be all the more convincing if you can demonstrate the skills and personal qualities you have. Working through the stages of the career planning process will help you to identify the particular strengths and experience that you have to offer and to target jobs and opportunities which match your needs and aspirations.

- *be used no matter what your situation.* The early retirer, the mid-career changer and the new graduate can all use the career planning process. It is a universally applicable way of making a job or career move, deciding on the kinds of activity in which you would like to become involved. Whether you aspire to freelance or part time work, voluntary or paid work, the process can be adopted at any time to assist you with your decision-making.

- *often be an iterative process,* which means that you may have to repeat it more than once to find a suitable work or study option. You may find, for example, that having worked through the exercises, the idea of further study is an option which most appeals, only to discover that the fees involved are prohibitively expensive and you have to reconsider your options by restarting the process.

The diagram on page 28 illustrates the various activities involved in the process and the sequence usually adopted.

There is, of course, a downside. Career planning can prove very time consuming. Exhaustive information search and protracted personal review can absorb considerable time and energy, which makes it difficult for those in work to engage in the process, as well as those coping with a study workload. No wonder many people would prefer to visit a clairvoyant. This applies particularly to what is known as 'creative job search', when the onus is on you to research a range of possible job or career options rather than simply to respond to classified job advertisements as they appear in the press. There can, however, be dividends, as one PhD student acknowledged:

> *I was just finishing my doctorate in physics and I hadn't a clue what I wanted to do. I knew though, that I wasn't destined for a career in scientific research. One day I was just reading through a booklet on careers for scientists and I saw it mentioned – scientific journalism. I hadn't considered the idea before, but instinctively I knew that was what I wanted to do. It fitted . . . I'd really like to work on 'Tomorrow's World'!*

## CAREER PLANNING: THE STEPS YOU NEED TO TAKE

In order to decide what you want to do in career terms, you need to work through one very simple process – career planning. It is not, as the term might imply, a question of planning your life away, but simply a way of sorting out your immediate goals, of deciding what to do next in your career. And the process can be used no matter at what stage you are in your life: for changing career, for initial career plans, for any career decision.

What's involved? Simply follow the stages outlined below and you should arrive at some answers to questions such as: What career am I suited for? What options are open to me? How can I go about deciding?

CAREER PLANNING: STEPS IN THE PROCESS

| **Assessing yourself** | Identify your values, skills, interests and other personal attributes.<br>Review your previous experience.<br>Describe your findings in the form of a summary statement or record. |
|---|---|
| **Researching ideas and opportunities** | Envision future opportunities.<br>Seek and assess relevant information.<br>Identify sources of help and support. |

*continued*

— *continued* – – – – – – – – – – – – – – – – – – – – – –

| **Making connections** | Gain feedback on your ideas for your career development. Identify personal priorities and constraints. Integrate self-assessment findings with options available to you. |
| **Taking action** | Write and carry out an action plan. Communicate effectively both orally and in writing to achieve objectives. Review your progress and identify the learning points for your future career planning. |

## ASSESSING YOURSELF

This is the first essential step in the career planning process and for many people the most difficult, raising a host of questions. How do I go about it? What criteria do I use? Who do I compare myself with?

Briefly stated there are three main criteria which are vital for career planning, a knowledge of:

- your abilities and skills, e.g. problem-solving, communicating;
- your interests, e.g. the environment, music, sport;
- your values, e.g. wanting to be successful, wanting to help other people.

In this process you are not necessarily making comparisons between yourself and others but *intrapersonally*, that is, comparing your range of skills and interests to see which are the more important. There are various ways in which you can accomplish the task. You can review your previous experience to identify your particular interests and strengths. You can use a variety of questionnaires or computer-assisted guidance systems. You can also ask other people for their impressions of your personality and values. Getting personal feedback of this kind may be surprising, even painful, but it will certainly be illuminating. There are various ways in which to undertake this process of personal review and reflection, and it's best to use a variety of ways to find some consistent answers.

When you have made some progress, it's useful to summarize your findings in a *personal and career profile* which lists all the things about you which are relevant to your career decision. You might find, for example, that you definitely want to use your qualifications in some way, or that the skills you have developed in the workplace are ones that you want to develop further. You may find that some previous unpaid or leisure experience will be particularly useful in shaping your future career plan.

## ❏ Case Study: Jane
*Before going to university, Jane had worked in a marketing and PR department and therefore knew something of the process of promoting products to a particular market. During her Italian degree, she'd spent some time teaching English as a foreign language (TEFL) in Italy and desperately wanted to return there after graduating. When she saw a job vacancy with an English publisher of TEFL materials for a marketing representative in Northern Italy, she felt she had something to offer!*

Making the connections between your experience, skills and interests can help you define your career plans more clearly and confidently. There are, however, some difficulties and problems you may encounter.

*'How do I know if I'm good at something if I've never tried it?'*

This is a very real problem for would be self-assessors. It's obviously very difficult to assess your skills and competencies in activities which you haven't yet tried. The only thing you can do is to project yourself into a given situation and think about the way you might perform. Or, much better, find a situation in which you can try yourself out! Voluntary or short term work is invaluable in crystallizing your career plans.

*'The things which interest me have no career relevance or offer no immediate job prospects.'*

Even if you can't see the relevance of your interests to a job or career, it's still important to acknowledge them. Firstly, because you may want to develop them in non-work settings. Painting or writing creatively for yourself may well assume an importance equal to or greater than the work you do for a living. Secondly, you may not be able to see the relevance now, but there may well be opportunities in the future which you are not able to predict.

There are plenty of instances of people's leisure activities taking over their lives completely and providing the basis for freelance work.

## RESEARCHING IDEAS

'Why is it that information for such an important life process as career planning and career decision making is often left to chance reading of newspapers or coincidental contacts with relatives or friends?'

The question is posed by an American careers expert, Frederickson (1982) and points to the very real problem that many career decisions are made on the basis of scant or inadequate information which often provides for unsatisfactory outcomes. The task for effective career planners is therefore to use a wide range of information which enables them to gain the best possible understanding of careers or employers and, indeed, test the reality of different options before committing themselves to a particular career idea. In your information search there are two aspects you will need to consider – information type and information search method.

## TYPE OF INFORMATION

At a general level you can assemble data about job market trends which may have a bearing on the number of opportunities open to you. Anyone thinking about investing time in training or development will want to take this kind of information into account. There is some risk in investing your time and money in training if jobs don't exist in the area for which you are being trained. Another kind of query might concern the availability of local work.

If you're tied to a particular geographical area, you will need to identify prospects in the local labour market.

Occupational information in the form of descriptions of what's involved in different jobs, entry requirements, qualifications needed, salaries etc. will need to be considered alongside details of prospective employers and potential vacancies. You may also identify training needs and want to research opportunities for further study and training.

## SEARCH METHODS

A good deal of information we have about careers and the job market comes from secondary sources: friends, newspaper articles and TV programmes.

Most job seekers are therefore faced with sometimes out-of-date, sometimes incomplete, often unreliable data about careers and job opportunities. It's no wonder, therefore, that job seekers make stereotypical assumptions about the options that are available to them and the demands of particular employers in terms of entry requirements. A typical assumption would be that, because there are over two million unemployed, any job vacancy is going to have two million potential applications and that there's little point in applying. This is, of course, a fallacy. If you rely on primary sources, you are more likely to gain a realistic view of the job market in a given geographical area or for a particular occupation. Primary sources such as employers, personal contacts, and people engaged in working in a particular job are more likely to give you the 'insider' view which not only helps you in your career decision making, but also gives you immediate, first-hand assessment of your prospects. Approaches based on creative job search and informational interviewing in which you target individuals who can be of help to you are time consuming, but offer considerable potential. An introduction to informational interviewing can be found in Chapter 6.

Having stressed the value of firsthand information there are none the less a large number of secondary sources which are extremely valuable.

Details of different kinds of work can be found in careers guides and computer software. Information about employers is given in the employer directories and employers will provide their own brochures. Data on employment prospects, including salary information and job market trends are also available. Details of vacancies can be found in the local and national media as well as in professional journals. Compendia of postgraduate courses provide details of all the UK courses at postgraduate level.

## MAKING CONNECTIONS

The third stage involves drawing together the results of your self-assessment and your research on the available options. Often referred to as 'decision-making', this stage is far more concerned with a synthesizing of data about yourself and potential career areas. It could, of course, result in a choice of one or more potential options, but the task is often greater than simply choosing between different alternatives. It may involve you in a range of activities which help to clarify your career thinking.

This could involve you in looking for feedback on your ideas from other people, or checking your ideas on your initial option list to research them in more detail.

The key task is to assess the options that seem appropriate in order to narrow down the range of possible options – a progressive focusing. If you are undecided about a particular option, or if you are faced with a choice between alternative options, there are a variety of strategies you can adopt:

- Seek further information. Many career searchers have only partial information about the options on offer. Additional information makes the decision easier.

- Gain feedback on your decision. Talking about your ideas to a good listener will always help you clarify your decision.

- Carry out a weighting exercise. Choose a particular criterion, e.g. starting salary, and see how the options compare. Weighting your options against various criteria forms the basis of many computer-assisted career decision-making systems.

- Make a balance sheet. For each career option you are considering draw two columns on a sheet of paper; on the left side list all the positive points about a particular option and on the right hand side all the drawbacks. You can refine this still further by considering the positive and negative consequences of your career decisions.

In the end, of course, your decision will have to be made and it may mean leaving your options open until you gauge your success in applying. This is why many people leave their options open and apply for several possible openings in the hope that their decision will become clearer over time. In this way the selection process you go through can provide a useful test of your commitment to one option or another. Putting your ideas to the test will often help to focus your mind very clearly.

DECISION SUMMARY

| |
|---|
| On the basis of your self-assessment, what are the important factors in your career decision? |
| On the basis of your research, what are the options which seem to fit? |

## SETTING GOALS AND PLANNING THE ACTION YOU ARE GOING TO TAKE

Being clear about what you want to do is a vital part of the career planning process because it can increase your sense of purpose and self-confidence. If you feel trapped by feelings of inertia and self-doubt, having goals to aim for can help you feel more optimistic about the future and encourage you to take more control of your life. This is one of the aims of the goal setting and action planning. What does this involve? In particular there are two simple questions you will need to ask yourself: 'Where am I going to go with my life?' and 'How am I going to get there?'

When you have carried out your personal review and researched some of the career options you can proceed with the process of goal setting by completing the following question boxes.

| |
|---|
| What is your preferred career goal? |
| By when might you hope to have achieved this? |

It's quite likely that in thinking of career options and putting them into practice there will be some factors which help you on your way, and at the same time obstacles to progress. The next step, therefore, is to undertake a force-field analysis to list all the things that are going to work towards this goal and those things which are going to work against you. Try to list at least six items under each heading, being as specific as you can. Identifying these positive and negative forces will help you see what you need to do to achieve your goal, and also recognize and gain confidence from things operating in your favour.

| Positive forces<br>e.g. degree qualification | Negative forces<br>e.g. lack of direct experience |
| --- | --- |
| 1. | 1. |
| 2. | 2. |
| 3. | 3. |
| 4. | 4. |
| 5. | 5. |
| 6. | 6. |

Finally, your plan of action should identify what you are going to do to achieve your goal(s), when you are going to complete the tasks and who can help you in this process. In particular, your action plan should also indicate how you are going to strengthen the positive forces mentioned above and overcome some of the negative factors affecting your career goal. You might, for example, see lack of relevant experience as a negative factor in achieving your career goal but you could overcome this by:

- doing a postgraduate course with a vocational emphasis

- finding voluntary work

- working on a short-term contract to gain temporary experience.

If you find it difficult to state one career goal, it's possible to list a couple of options and, in your action plan, describe ways in which you will choose one or the other.

You may also need to distinguish between short- and long-term goals. One final and important question to ask yourself is 'How will I know when I have achieved my goal?'

## YOUR ACTION PLAN

| Steps I need to take | Who can help? | By when? |
|---|---|---|
|  |  |  |

## COMMUNICATING EFFECTIVELY

Whatever action plan you decide on, you will invariably have to communicate with other people to put it into practice. Some examples of this kind of activity might include:

- getting in touch with family or friends who can help with information and advice;

- producing a well written curriculum vitae;

- targeting possible employers with a speculative letter together with your CV;

- approaching alumni or other contacts to carry out 'informational' interviews;

- responding to job advertisements to obtain the maximum amount of information about the job and the employer;

- making a presentation at a job selection interview.

The same process will apply equally to those applying for postgraduate courses or research posts, 'stages' or other forms of temporary or short-term work experience.

In the main it will be your task to convince other people that you can achieve whatever goals you have set yourself, whether it's a job or further training, further study or research. Most job seekers are notoriously reticent in promoting themselves to a potential employer and fail to prepare themselves for the selection process. In addition to completing the formal application you could also be:

- approaching similar employers to get an idea of the way they operate;

- ensuring that you have a job description and job details;

- making contact with people who already do the kind of work you want;

- talking to staff in the organization to which you are applying.

Above all, you should be consciously developing your own personal network of contacts so that you will get to know of future work opportunities as they arise.

## MAKING A START

This summary of the career planning process is designed to provide an overview of the steps you need to take in choosing or changing a career. The following chapter will take you through the first part of the process, self-assessment, inviting you to build up your own personal career development profile. The following chapters should give you an idea of the range of ways in which you can decide on and implement your career plans. To begin the process of personal review it will be helpful to put something on paper about yourself – a statement of your experience to date, however long or short.

## YOUR CAREER BIOGRAPHY

A number of writers now stress the importance of biography work in developing your career (Fritchie, 1990). Simply stated, this means writing about your career and personal development to date as a precursor to future planning. Particularly appropriate for people with some work experience behind them, the approach can be useful for anyone who has been made redundant, who wants to make a mid-career change or is returning to work after a career break. While there may be considerable benefits in working on your biography in a workshop or support group, it's perfectly possible to work on your autobiography in the comparative comfort of your own home and you can make a start by simply writing about any aspect of your previous work life. Fritchie, however, recommends users of the approach to start with seven strategy questions to provide a framework for the writing.

1. Where are you? (Describe fully your current life stage, both personal and career.)

2. How did you get there? (Look back at your life and trace all the elements, happenings and people that have influenced your life path.)

3. Where do you want to go? (Using the material from questions 1 and 2 begin to describe your real intentions.)

4. How will you get there? (Refer to the information you have gained about your journey in life so far and consider new ways.)

5. What will you do when you arrive? (Begin to sketch in your intentions and actions.)

6. Where to next? (Life is a continuous process, therefore it is important to begin to look beyond your immediate horizons.)

7. How do you begin?

Once you have started you can begin to review what you've written to pick out particular themes or critical incidents. From the career planning perspective some issues will be particularly significant. For example, when did you feel happiest or most stimulated by the work you were doing? What activities did you particularly enjoy? What tasks did you dislike doing? When doing this it will be particularly useful to try to identify times when you felt most spontaneous and in touch with your true self. Abraham Maslow referred to these occasions as 'peak experiences', times when individuals typically use their abilities to the full and as a result gain a great deal of satisfaction from their work.

You can also ask yourself a further range of questions which will be helpful to see how you have approached career issues in the past. How did you reach previous career decisions? Who were your mentors in the early stages of your career and how did they influence your development? What domestic and other constraints were operating at the time? How did the work affect your lifestyle?

If you find the idea of writing your autobiography too large a task or too open-ended, it may help to focus on one particular job or chapter in your life. Use the profile postscript at the end of the next chapter to provide you with a framework. Completing your career biography will be a useful preparation for the following chapter and also enable you to identify some of the key experiences of your career to date.

# Chapter Three

# *Your Personal and Career Profile*

*Why did I decide to be a writer? As a child, I had never taken my scribblings seriously; my real aim had been to acquire knowledge. I enjoyed doing French compositions, but my teachers objected to my stilted style; I did not feel I was a 'born' writer. Yet at the age of fifteen when I wrote in a friend's album the plans and preferences which were supposed to give a picture of my personality, I answered without hesitation the question 'What do you want to do later in life?' with 'To be a famous author.'*

Simone de Beauvoir *Memoirs of a Dutiful Daughter*

In working on your career autobiography, or at least part of it, you may already have been able to observe particular patterns in your work history, in the way you respond to work situations, or in the ways in which you have coped with choices and change in the past. The aim of this chapter is to provide you with the opportunity for a structured self-appraisal, to give you some further insights into your career needs and to build a personal profile which will be an essential reference point for any future career decisions.

The process is important and potentially productive for a number of reasons:

* As the quotation from Simone de Beauvoir shows, it can offer self-understanding and insight by revealing thoughts and ideas which we may have been harbouring semi-consciously but have never before expressed or articulated. Very often it is not necessarily the results of your self-appraisal which are significant, but the mere process of thinking about the issues which helps to generate ideas, offer insights and provide a stimulus for action. All too often we carry around with us hopes and ideas for our

own futures, but fail to commit the ideas to paper or turn them into reality, simply because we haven't time to consider them at length. Sometimes we simply lack confidence in asserting them. Consequently, some of our best and most imaginative ideas fail to see the light of day. It is only when we give ourselves the opportunity to discuss or describe our ideas that they begin to take shape and assume a more tangible form.

• It helps one to reflect on experience. One of the crucial stages of the learning cycle is that of review and reflection, but we seldom give ourselves enough time to reflect on previous experience and learn from our past actions before we identify options for change or development.

• At a pragmatic level, completing the following questionnaires will also provide you with considerable raw data for your curriculum vitae and enable you to answer some of the more awkward questions you may find on application forms or encounter at interview, for example 'What have you achieved in your career to date?' or 'Why are you applying for this particular job?' Commonly many jobseekers 'undersell' the value of their skills and experience to potential employers. They often fail to provide a full and positive description of their work and educational experience. By completing the following questionnaires you will, at least, have some definite descriptions of your achievements and interests which you can use to good effect when promoting yourself.

• Finally, the review process you undertake will develop your skills in self-appraisal so that you can repeat it at various stages in your future. Career planning is iterative; it is a process we constantly revisit. If your initial ideas for change don't come to fruition you will need to reconsider and revisit the results of your appraisal. If your ideal choice of career is one that seems unattainable given the limitations of the job market, you may need to return to look at other options. Self-appraisal and self-assessment are skills which we need to acquire in order to make career decisions effectively. We have to work at our ability to see ourselves. This is not simply idle speculation. As Bannister (1982) argues:

> *To try and understand oneself is not simply an interesting pastime, it is a necessity of life. In order to plan our future and to make choices we have to be able to anticipate our behaviour in future*

*situations This makes self-knowledge a practical guide, not a self-indulgence.*

The following questionnaires have been designed to take you in a structured way through the self-appraisal stage of the career planning process. Your answers will provide the basis for your personal and career profile in a summary statement which records your career experience.

Some people, it has to be acknowledged, have concerns about the idea of any form of self-assessment. In particular they need to know which yardstick to use for comparison purposes. Their friends or family? Fellow workmates? In each of the questionnaires which follow, you will be asked to make some kind of review and appraisal of personal qualities and attitudes. Try, where possible, not to look for comparisons between yourself and other people but instead look for intrapersonal comparisons. In assessing your skills, for example, there are inevitably going to be some things at which you are more skilled than others. For the purposes of career planning, *your* view of your skills and competencies is the most important factor in shaping your future goals. Obviously, it is very illuminating to have other people's perceptions of your strengths and the skills you need to develop further. For the purpose of the following questionnaires, however, we are concerned very largely with your own self-appraisal.

## IDENTIFYING YOUR WORK VALUES

We all have needs that we hope will be satisfied in our working lives. Most people expect sufficient economic return for their efforts and some recognition for the contribution of their time and energy spent in the workplace. And it's possible to recognize that, in working, people are progressively trying to meet a hierarchy of needs. At a basic level we work to satisfy our need for food and shelter but once these needs are satisfied we strive for higher-order needs concerned with personal fulfilment and what Maslow termed 'self-actualisation'.

It is also evident that people have different sets of personal values and therefore what we value in work will differ, as will our prime motive for wanting to work in one career area rather than another. Nurses, social workers and teachers are often motivated by the idea of working at something of social value; senior managers in industry may be driven more by the idea of the

## MY WORK VALUES

**Score**
6 = most important; 1 = least important

I want a job where . . .

| | | |
|---|---|---|
| . . . I can get ahead in my career | (A) | . . . |
| . . . I can help people cope better with their lives | (Su) | . . . |
| . . . there is a high financial reward | (E) | . . . |
| . . . job security is guaranteed | (Se) | . . . |
| . . . I can work independently of others | (I) | . . . |
| . . . I can do things which involve some risk | (R) | . . . |
| . . . I can enjoy high social status | (P) | . . . |
| . . . there is quite a bit of travel involved | (V) | . . . |
| . . . I can enjoy my place of work | (En) | . . . |
| . . . I can do work that is socially useful | (Su) | . . . |
| . . . I can develop new ideas or products | (C) | . . . |
| . . . there is little work-related stress | (Se) | . . . |
| . . . people respect me for my position | (P) | . . . |
| . . . there is plenty of scope for advancement | (A) | . . . |
| . . . there are new challenges and ventures | (R) | . . . |
| . . . things are left entirely to my own judgement | (I) | . . . |
| . . . there is a pleasant working environment | (En) | . . . |
| . . . I am in charge of other people | (Au) | . . . |
| . . . I can work as part of a team | (S) | . . . |
| . . . I can be creative or inventive | (C) | . . . |
| . . . a very good standard of living is possible | (E) | . . . |
| . . . there are friendly people around me | (S) | . . . |
| . . . there is a lot of variety in what I do | (V) | . . . |
| . . . I have the authority to get things done | (Au) | . . . |

# *SCORE SHEET*

| Value | Score |
|---|---|
| ADVANCEMENT (*A*)<br>Upward mobility and promotion.<br>More interesting work. | ☐ |
| SOCIAL (*S*)<br>Friendly contact with workmates.<br>Attending to and talking with people. | ☐ |
| ECONOMIC (*E*)<br>High salary and financial rewards. | ☐ |
| SECURITY (*Se*)<br>Job stability and regular income.<br>No threat to economic or social well-being. | ☐ |
| INDEPENDENCE (*I*)<br>Autonomy – freedom to make decisions<br>and take the initiative. | ☐ |
| PRESTIGE (*P*)<br>Being seen in an important role.<br>Social, economic or occupational status. | ☐ |
| VARIETY (*V*)<br>Change and variety in task and place of work.<br>The opportunity to train. | ☐ |
| ENVIRONMENT (*En*)<br>Pleasant physical surroundings. | ☐ |
| SUPPORT (*Su*)<br>Helping people.<br>Work of social or community value. | ☐ |
| CREATIVE (*C*)<br>Being original and dealing with new ideas.<br>Creating new products.<br>Finding different solutions to problems. | ☐ |
| RISK (*R*)<br>An element of uncertainty.<br>Financial and other kinds of risk. | ☐ |
| AUTHORITY (*Au*)<br>Influence and control over other people.<br>Leading others and making decisions. | ☐ |

economic return for their work or the prestige they gain from their position; entrepreneurs, by the risk and uncertainty offered by business activities.

Often, in response to the crisis of mid-life described earlier, our values come up for review. What previously had seemed to give us a psychological return from our work no longer does so. We question the values that guided us at earlier stages in our career and look for a career change which will bring into play a different set of personal values. Our values and needs may change with time. Major life events, such as the birth of a child, divorce or bereavement may all trigger a review and re-ordering of our personal priorities.

The aim of the questionnaire which follows is to invite you to order a number of different value statements in terms of their relevance to you.

Give a score of 6 to those values which are *very important* to you and a score of 1 to those which appear *largely unimportant* in your case.

When you have finished, you can add up the scores with a similar code and transfer the totals to your score sheet.

## INTERPRETING YOUR SCORES

You may find it difficult to identify one or two value statements to which you can attach more importance than others and want elements of all of these to be expressed in your work time. It's more likely, however, that you will attach greater importance to some statements than to others.

Your rank order will have particular significance if you are planning a career choice or change. For example, which values will you trade off against the others in anticipating a change of career direction? How will the risk and uncertainty of working for yourself as a freelance square with your apparent need for security? How will you reconcile a sideways career move with the value you place on the need for status enhancement? Your work values may well determine the content of your work, your work style and the aims of the organization you work for, and any career choice or change will bring value questions into play. Unwitting adherence to one particular set of values may also block or hinder forms of personal and career development. As one American careers writer put it, 'Most folks dance the Safety, Security, Longevity Polka. Security is the usual trade-off for work a person regards as dull, routine and meaningless'. Issues concerned with personal development will be addressed later in Chapter 5, but at this point it is worth highlighting that many of us have perhaps one or two guiding value constants which underpin our working experience and which shape the overall direction of our careers. Edgar Schein used the term 'career anchors' to describe 'patterns of self-perceived talents, motives and values' which guide, constrain, stabilize and integrate the person's career. His longitudinal study of management school alumni led him to identify a set of eight career anchors which were reflected in individual career histories. Career anchors, Schein argues, are developed as a result of work experience and relate very clearly to the occupational self-concept of Super's theory of career development. They represent the personal values 'you would not give up if you were forced to make a choice' in addition to your self-perceptions of needs and skills.

---

### CAREER ANCHORS

**Technical functional competence** – wanting to exercise your skills in one particular field e.g. finance, personnel, teaching, engineering

**Managerial competence** – wanting to co-ordinate the work of other people

**Autonomy/independence** – wanting to keep as free as possible from organizational rules and restrictions and set your own agenda

**Sense of service** – wanting to exercise your sense of altruism

**Pure challenge** – you want variety, novelty, to surmount difficult obstacles and to win

**Lifestyle integration** – wanting to make all parts of your life into an integrated whole

**Entrepreneurship** – your main concern is to create something new, engage in a new venture

**Security/stability** – your primary concern is financial security and geographical stability

# YOUR PERSONAL SKILLS

Skills, talents, abilities – define them as you will, they are essential ingredients in the process of deciding on career options. Most people choose careers which are consistent with their own ability profile. They are motivated to find the kind of work they can do best. For some individuals, one particular skill overrides all others and takes on the status of a leitmotif. Painter Norman Rockwell describes how at the age of 12 he decided to become an illustrator. 'Boys who were athletes were expressing themselves fully, they had an identity, a recognized place among other boys. All I had was the ability to draw. Because it was all I had, I made it my whole life . . . I drew and drew and drew.' Others among us will find it less easy to identify one particular skill which will serve us throughout life, and will use a range of skills in our work and leisure time. The aim of the skills checklist is to help you assess which of your personal skills are the most important to you and to review the career implications of your skills profile. When you have completed your scores, you can see which group of occupations matches your main skills.

## WHAT KIND OF SKILLS?

It is helpful to distinguish between three sets of skills. Skills in *self-management* are those which we all need to be effective in our everyday lives, in studying successfully, in coping with competing demands on our time. Examples of self-management skills include time-management, managing stress, coping with personal change. These skills are essential for everyone and are necessary for any job, career or kind of work. *Career planning* skills are those that are typically used in choosing and changing careers and deciding on development options. Once you have been through career planning activities, they become easier to repeat at successive stages in your career. These were described in the previous chapter. The skills checklist is concerned with your *core skills* – those skills which you are likely to use in your work more than others. Skills such as problem-solving or communicating effectively or data handling. Of course, some of the core skills are skills that you need for self-management and career planning.

Why is the process of identifying skills important? As most professionals involved in careers counselling will attest, most of us are notoriously reticent about describing what we can do and seeing the relevance of our skills to the workplace. In part this is perhaps because we trivialize skills and denigrate their importance, associating them with routine everyday tasks. 'Listening to people' or 'organizing events' may on the face of it appear to have little occupational significance, but on the other hand ... In order to counter this we need to recognize a significant feature of skills – that they are transferable from job to job, one occupational setting to another. Being aware of this transferability of personal skills is therefore a key factor in maintaining a sense of self-worth and career confidence, and in promoting ourselves effectively. Read through the following checklist of skills and give yourself a score from 1 to 5 (1 = not at all like me, 5 = very like me)

## CORE SKILLS CHECKLIST

*WORKING CREATIVELY*

designing ☐

visualizing ☐ Your total for working creatively ☐

generating new ideas ☐

performing ☐

making artefacts ☐

*HANDLING NUMERICAL DATA*

calculating ☐

estimating costs ☐ Your total for handling numerical ☐

budgeting ☐    data

accounting ☐

valuing and pricing ☐

*WORKING WITH TEXT*

writing ☐

reporting ☐ Your total for working with text ☐

editing ☐

translating ☐

ability to précis ☐

PRACTICAL COMPETENCE

using equipment ☐

working with materials ☐ Your total for practical ☐
competence

working with plants or ☐
animals

building/constructing ☐

assembling components ☐


PROBLEM-SOLVING

analysing information ☐

lateral thinking ☐ Your total for problem-solving ☐

finding solutions ☐

interpreting charts and ☐
diagrams

diagnosing faults ☐


ORGANIZING

arranging events ☐

working to deadlines ☐ Your total for organizing ☐

setting priorities ☐

managing meetings ☐

scheduling activities ☐


CARRYING OUT RESEARCH

seeking information ☐

analysing data ☐ Your total for carrying out ☐
research

observing/recording ☐

interpreting findings ☐

sampling ☐

*RELATING TO PEOPLE*

listening ☐
interviewing ☐ Your total for relating to people ☐
showing understanding ☐
working co-operatively ☐
coaching others ☐

*INFLUENCING*

negotiating agreement ☐
selling a product ☐ Your total for influencing ☐
leading others ☐
networking ☐
motivating people ☐

*COMMUNICATING*

explaining facts ☐
presenting information ☐ Your total for communicating ☐
expressing ideas ☐
making proposals ☐
providing advice ☐

## CORE SKILL SCORE SHEET

Under the following headings, fill in the total for each of the skill headings. When you have entered all the scores, you can rank your skills in order from the highest to the lowest scores and in the following pages assess the implications of your skill scores for your career decision.

|  | Total score | Rank order |
| --- | --- | --- |
| Working creatively | ☐ | ☐ |
| Handling numerical data | ☐ | ☐ |
| Working with text | ☐ | ☐ |
| Practical competence | ☐ | ☐ |
| Problem-solving | ☐ | ☐ |

CORE SKILL SCORE SHEET (*continued*)

|  | Total score | Rank order |
|---|---|---|
| Organizing | ☐ | ☐ |
| Carrying out research | ☐ | ☐ |
| Relating to people | ☐ | ☐ |
| Influencing | ☐ | ☐ |
| Communicating | ☐ | ☐ |

---

Additional skills I have developed:




On reflection, skills I would like to develop further:




---

## INTERPRETING YOUR SKILL SCORES

In reviewing your skill scores, you will probably find that one or two of the skills mentioned below will have particular relevance to your choice of career and the kind of work you will do in future. You will also be able to identify your skill gaps, areas you might want to develop or which are not important to you in your future career. In interpreting the results, you will need to bear in mind three points in particular. Firstly, most jobs will involve a range of skills, all important to a greater or lesser extent. A maths teacher, for example, will need to communicate effectively, handle numerical data, be able to relate to pupils and write reports on their progress (among other things!). Secondly, skills are capable of development. You may be good at activities that you haven't yet tried and will just need some additional training to improve your performance. Finally, you may have skills which you may not need in your job, but that you will develop in your 'leisure' or outside work activities The airline pilot involved in amateur theatricals, the accountant who plays in a jazz band, the physiotherapist who also does antique restoration are all examples of individuals using skills and developing interests in non-work settings.

## WORKING WITH TEXT
Editorial staff, print journalists, indexers and proof-readers, scriptwriters and advertising copywriters all have work which revolves around the printed word. Anyone who has experience of putting together a journal or magazine will recognize the range of text processing skills required. Many jobs involve skills in written communication. Educational administrators, Foreign Office desk staff and all secretaries need these skills. They are also a central feature of many information officer and public relations jobs in the public and private sector, as well as the third or not-for-profit sector.

## WORKING CREATIVELY
Designers of graphics, furniture and textiles will naturally use this range of skills, as will architects and interior designers. It will provide the main focus of their work and vocational training. It is interesting also to see how relevant this skill can be to a range of other career areas open to graduates of other subjects e.g. advertising copywriter, landscape architect, arts administrator, as well as engineering specialisms concerned with design.

## RELATING TO PEOPLE
Counsellors, social workers, guidance and advice-centre workers will all need these skills in varying degrees, as well as all professional psychologists who are involved in diagnosis, assessment and therapy. A wide range of training courses exists to develop these skills further, something which can also be achieved by volunteer experience and related part-time work.

## CARRYING OUT RESEARCH
Many professional jobs have an evaluation or research element, but research workers of all kinds will, needless to say, use their research skills as a main element in their work. Whether research into social issues, for market research, for trade unions or government departments or management consultants – a set of core skills is essential. In general, jobs which involve information processing require these skills, e.g. librarians, information workers, as well as jobs which involve some form of survey or other research activity.

## PRACTICAL COMPETENCE

Jobs which are centred on the use of equipment and hardware necessarily require these skills. Traditionally associated with manual crafts, this skill is also required at higher technical and scientific levels and in some aspects of information technology. The medical laboratory technician, the sound engineer in a recording studio, the archaeologist, the museum curator, the wildlife conservationist all need practical skills in their work.

## ORGANIZING

All administrators and managers need to organize events and meetings. They make things happen. Indeed, these are the skills associated with management activities, common to a wide variety of different careers; arts administrators, conference organizers, sales managers.

## PROBLEM-SOLVING

Engineers of all kinds, computer programmers and systems analysts all need problem-solving skills, finding solutions to technical problems.

## COMMUNICATING

It is difficult to be precise about the range of jobs available under this heading as there are so many. Teachers communicate, but then so do journalists, especially broadcast journalists, who communicate to an audience. Housing managers and marketing executives do it. So do TV researchers, interpreters, conference organizers, sales staff, agricultural advisers and advertising staff, and all manner of consultants, trainers and managers require these skills in abundance.

## HANDLING NUMERICAL DATA

Engineers and scientific researchers of all kinds require this skill along with other professionals – statisticians, actuaries, maths teachers, transportation planners and operational researchers. Perhaps surprisingly, this is only a secondary skill for accountants – communicating comes first! It's an important skill, but by no means the essential skill for many jobs in the financial sector.

## INFLUENCING

Many managers will have skills in this area, so it's a skill area common to a wide range of jobs of this kind. Marketing and sales staff will also exhibit this skill *par excellence*, as well as estate agents, surveyors, advertising account executives, secondary school teachers, solicitors and, above all, barristers. Police officers and production managers, in particular, rely on their powers of persuasion in carrying out their work.

## YOUR WORK INTERESTS

Occupational psychologists have developed a range of tests and questionnaires which measure individual interests. The scores have been found to be reasonably good predictors of career choices. Certainly, various studies have shown that people in similar occupations can have a clearly identifiable interest profile, and interest questionnaires have been widely used in research studies of the work interests of different occupation groups.

Interests are, of course, one aspect of personality, and have proved to be a popular indicator because of the ease with which interests can be assessed. They also enable users to state preferences for one kind of work rather than another, irrespective of their particular abilities or skills and for this reason are widely used for individual career planning and, on occasion, for job selection.

For those unused to self-appraisal, the thought of stating preferences for different kinds of work activity is often hedged with qualification. 'How can I say I'm interested in something if I've never tried it?' is a fairly typical response. For the purposes of the following exercise simply rate the items in terms of whether they seem, on the face of it, to hold any interest for you. Try not to think about whether you could do them successfully. Merely express your interest at this stage, and try not to agonize over each item. Your initial response is probably the most significant for this exercise. There are 48 items in all, and you have to rate each statement, giving it a score for the degree of interest it holds for you, from 5 (this interests me a lot) to 1 (this doesn't interest me at all).

Write reports on political events in Third World countries ☐ C

Look after the rights and welfare of tenants on a housing estate ☐ S

Design the packaging for the launch of a new product ☐ D

Plan the control of occupational and environmental radiation hazards ☐ I

Set up a network of personal computers ☐ P

Specify new procedures for collecting a company's sales data ☐ M

Work as a freelance business adviser ☐ E

Prepare tax returns for self-employed workers ☐ N


Translate promotional literature for exported goods ☐ C

Advise young people on the choices for further study and training ☐ S

Provide art or music therapy for children ☐ D

Carry out circuit design on flight simulators and trainers ☐ I

Test computer software for educational use ☐ P

Establish a telephone helpline for handling customer enquiries ☐ M

Estimate the value of houses and office premises ☐ E

Carry out a large-scale consumer survey ☐ N


Write press releases for a charity oranization ☐ C

Help people cope with high levels of stress ☐ S

Design audio-visual teaching and training aids ☐ D

Test the sensitivity of the human ear to harmonic distortion ☐ I

Grow glasshouse flowers and vegetable produce ☐ P

Advise hoteliers and small businesses on how to attract tourists ☐ M

Promote sales of products at exhibitions and trade fairs ☐ E

Analyse the costs of a new computer system ☐ N

| | |
|---|---|
| Edit articles for magazines and journals | ☐ C |
| Find short-term accommodation for homeless families | ☐ S |
| Perform in 'theatre in education' or community arts projects | ☐ D |
| Carry out seismographic surveys for a mining company | ☐ I |
| Install air-conditioning in offices and shops | ☐ P |
| Interview applicants for clerical and administrative work | ☐ M |
| Arrange training placements in small and large companies | ☐ E |
| Assess applicants for business loans and overdrafts | ☐ N |
| | |
| Report on news and events for a local radio station | ☐ C |
| Teach English to groups of foreign students | ☐ S |
| Maintain and exhibit items in a natural history museum | ☐ D |
| Employ ultrasonics to test the thickness and flaw patterns of steel pipe | ☐ I |
| Work on irrigation schemes for developing countries | ☐ P |
| Purchase equipment and materials for an airline | ☐ M |
| Ensure that goods reach legal safety and quality standards | ☐ E |
| Analyse company accounts for investment purposes | ☐ N |
| | |
| Draft a commercial agreement between two companies | ☐ C |
| Work in a school for teenagers with emotional and behavioural problems | ☐ S |
| Plan and design kitchens and bathrooms | ☐ D |
| Chart the progress and absorption of drugs in the bloodstream | ☐ I |
| Build and design theatre sets | ☐ P |
| Organize tours and visits for parties of foreign tourists | ☐ M |
| Run a restaurant or wine bar | ☐ E |
| Design a research survey to test employee attitudes to training and appraisal | ☐ N |

INTEREST CATEGORIES SCORE SHEET

|  | Score | Rank Order |
|---|---|---|
| Communication (C) – writing and researching | | |
| Social (S) – helping and developing people | | |
| Design (D) – designing, creating and performing | | |
| Investigative (I) – working in science and technology | | |
| Practical (P) – making and working outdoors | | |
| Managing (M) – organizing and administration | | |
| Entrepreneurial (E) – persuading and being self-employed | | |
| Numerical (N) – using financial and research data | | |

# YOUR CAREER INTERESTS

We all enjoy work which matches our basic interests, and where possible we should therefore try to seek out career opportunities which match rather than conflict with our interest profile.

In reviewing your work interests checklist results, you will probably find that one or two of the interest areas mentioned below will have particular relevance in your career planning – usually those with the highest scores. You will also be able to identify fairly readily those interest areas that hold no appeal for you! It is also useful to look back on the high scores you have given to individual items in the profile, to identify particular interests. Brief descriptions or summaries of the different interest areas are given below. They should give you a general idea of the kind of work which might interest you most, perhaps confirming your existing career ideas.

*COMMUNICATION*
You have an interest in the written word and possibly in the process of research which accompanies 'reportage'. Media careers may appeal most but you might also look for other careers in business and industry which require written skills – research report writing, public relations, as well as work involving a legal emphasis.

## SOCIAL

Your work is likely to have a people focus motivated, perhaps, by your sense of altruism. The activities in this category are wide ranging – from teaching and advice-giving to direct helping intervention on behalf of other people. The extent of your people-involvement will depend on your particular values and skills, but it is likely that interpersonal skills will be of particular importance in this kind of career area.

## DESIGN

High scores in this area imply that you have dominant creative interests, whether in terms of design or performance. A key issue for most people is whether their creativity is a natural form of self-expression to be enjoyed in their non-work activities or whether it is to be a feature of paid employment/work/career. Yet again, creativity can find expression in your work style as well as in the kind of work you do.

## INVESTIGATIVE

Your interests are centred around scientific enquiry and the applications of technology. The work activities featured in the profile cover a wide range from engineering design and maintenance to biochemistry and so may not appear to be directly relevant given your particular qualification background.

However, what is important to establish in your career planning is the degree to which you are interested in using your technical problem-solving skills.

## PRACTICAL

Half of the items under this heading were concerned largely with the environment and outdoor activities which require considerable practical activity. The others require a different kind of activity concerned with practical problem-solving and in particular the ability to handle spatial relationships. Which kind of practical interests do you have and how do these manifest themselves?

## MANAGING

Activities under this heading all involve organizing activities, events and people. There is often a tendency for students to view 'management' as a serious career option for the middle-aged. In fact, many business and public sector careers involve some management responsibility, even at an early career stage.

*ENTREPRENEURIAL*

You either value the idea of working for yourself or show an interest in working in jobs which rely on your persuasiveness and negotiation skills. This doesn't imply just sales, but any work activity which involves marketing and promoting products and services.

*NUMERICAL*

Your main interests centre on data handling but from one of two perspectives – either financial data or that derived from the research process which might take the form of statistical output. It will be for you to decide which of these has the greater appeal and in particular to decide the degree to which you want to use your computational skills as well as your ability to draw inferences from the data in front of you.

In interpreting your interest scores two caveats need to be borne in mind. Firstly, you may be interested in a particular activity but not wish to express this interest in paid employment. It's perfectly possible, for example, to have a secure job, and exploit your entrepreneurial interests in your free or spare time; for example, to work indoors and spend your weekends doing environmental conservation work. Secondly, none of the activities listed may interest you particularly and you end up with a 'flat' profile. If this is the case you may like to make a note of activities which do interest you, listing as many as possible and seeing what implications they have for your future career development.

## MAKING EXPERIENCE WORK FOR YOU

Mark Twain's experience as a typesetter, and later as a river boat pilot, gave him both skills and material for his writing. 'One isn't a printer for ten years without setting up acres of good and bad literature and learning – unconsciously first, consciously later – to discriminate between the two.' Similarly, Dashiell Hammet's employment as a Pinkerton's detective provided the milieu for his central character, Sam Spade, in *The Maltese Falcon* as well as a string of other crime thrillers.

If you have had any previous work-related experience, paid or voluntary, full- or part-time, it can provide a basis for your future career changes and development. This is not to say that you will invariably end up doing the work that you have always done. Those wanting to change career direction because they are unhappy in their present work role will, of course, be anxious to make a fresh start and to try new areas of opportunity. Nevertheless, there will be elements of your previous experience which will assist you in the future. These may be personal skills, perhaps, that are transferable from one work setting to another or interests from your leisure or non-work activity which you can use as a basis for self-employment. Mid-career changers are often tempted to try to turn lifelong interests into a form of income-generating activity.

In reviewing your previous life experience, as you may have done in writing your work biography, try to assess, under the following headings, what you might have gained.

Your background knowledge

Particular products or processes?

Of different organizations?

Techniques that you are familiar with?

(Example: Anyone working voluntarily in a Citizens Advice Bureau is going to learn something about consumer or employment law.)

Personal skills you may have developed

Try to assess your interpersonal skills as well as any work place or technical skills.

(Example: Staff engaged in personnel or market research may have developed interviewing skills; line managers may have developed appraisal skills.)

Contacts made

Identify people who have been helpful to you in the past, as well as the sorts of people who can assist you in the future.

(Example: You may have found a mentor figure who has been particularly encouraging in your career to date.)

Lessons learned about yourself

> You may like to comment here about your attitudes to work, the way you cope with different tasks or the work settings in which you are most at home.
>
> (Example: Some of the events you may have experienced may well have given you an insight into your preferred work style.)

Your achievements to date

> These can be from any area of your life and, however great or small, can reflect events which have given you a sense of pleasure, success or reward.
>
> (Example: Gaining a professional qualification by part-time study whilst holding down a job.)

When you have completed your experience inventory, you may be surprised by the amount and range of your previous experience. And even if you feel like discounting elements of your past, it may be possible to draw on this reservoir of experience at some stage in the future. It will certainly provide a valuable addition to your personal and career development profile and, once again, give you material for your curriculum vitae.

## TIME AND PLACE: IDENTIFYING YOUR PERSONAL PRIORITIES

YOUR WORK LOCATION

Independently-minded careerists, free of constraints, just embarking on the first steps of their career may well be able to adopt an 'I'll go anywhere' approach to job search and be prepared to commit a large proportion of their daily lives to job and career. By contrast, women returners to the job market, dual career couples, single parents and those looking after dependent relatives may well wish to develop their careers in a given geographical area, investing a given proportion of their lives to paid employment while trying to balance other competing demands on their time. Some professionals, of course, may be quite content to see the entire world as their workplace. Civil engineers, for example, engaged on long- or short-term contracts abroad may well lead a largely expatriate lifestyle, in much the same way that Foreign Office staff are expected to do. Accountants and lawyers may also have the opportunity to work in the overseas offices of their parent companies.

Each of us will have different responses to make to the question 'Where would you like to work?' The following prompts are intended to help you clarify your priorities, if you are faced with a complete job change or relocation.

---

Ideally, I would like my work to be located in . . .

As a compromise, I would be content to work within the following geographical areas

At most, my travel time to work would be . . .

If asked to relocate with an employer, I would . . .

---

## WORK TIME

Freelancers and the self-employed enjoy more flexibility than others in achieving a balance between their work time, their discretionary time which can be given to leisure, educational or other activities, and their maintenance time which for most of us means rest and recuperation.

Those in full-time paid employment may have less flexibility but may be able to make some changes to their work pattern if they want to.

The more time we spend at work, the more we squeeze the other two. In making a choice of job and career it is therefore important to be clear about the amount of time we want to invest, so that we can achieve a balance. In addition, the way the working week is structured can vary tremendously from job to job: airline workers, hotel catering staff, nurses and police officers all have to cope with shift work of one kind or another. Many office workers, by contrast, are able to enjoy a certain amount of autonomy in the hours they work with flexitime arrangements. Many professional workers are expected to work overtime without additional salary; other workers will have nationally-agreed pay rates for overtime working. As we saw earlier, increasing numbers of jobs are being created on a part-time basis at the expense of full-time jobs. The amount of time we want to invest is, therefore, a key element in defining our ideal job.

Allied to the notion of time investment is our whole relationship with work itself. On the one hand some people see their working life as a segment of their lives which intrudes as little as possible on the mainstream of their existence. For others, life is work; consequently, work is a central component of their lifestyle and any distinction between work and leisure is meaningless. How do you view your preferred relationship with work? The questionnaire below provides you with the opportunity to review how much of your life you want to devote to work time.

## MY INVESTMENT IN WORK TIME

I couldn't possibly do something I wasn't interested in. There is no difference for me between work and leisure. My life is my work.

Work is an important part of my life and although it is not my sole reason for living, it certainly takes precedence over leisure, entertainment and non-work activities

I want to achieve some kind of balance between the energy I devote to work and that which I devote to non-work. Work and leisure are equally important.

Although I work reasonably hard while I am at work, when it comes to 5 p.m. I want to switch off. I refuse to take work home. My own time is very precious to me.

The kind of work I do has very little significance. All I want is the chance to earn enough to have a reasonable social/leisure/family life.

Which statement would you subscribe to? When you have found one which broadly represents your view, indicate the range of working hours which you can devote to paid employment in the relevant box.

## YOUR CAREER FANTASY

Many of us harbour seldom-articulated ideas about our future. 'Of course what I'd really like to do . . .' often prompts a revelation to those disclosing their innermost thoughts. Here is your chance to describe your ideal job, the work scenario that would provide the optimum fit between your hopes and aspirations and your personal circumstances. You need not restrict yourself to work/career ideas which fall within your grasp but allow yourself to envisage a future which you may not have already considered. Against each of the prompts below, try to describe as fully as you can the kind of elements you would like to find in your fantasy. It could offer some tantalizing insights into your future career direction.

1.  Ideally I would like to . . .
    (describe the activities in outline)

2.  It would make me feel good because . . .
    (describe the returns, the needs it would satisfy)

3.  It would interest me because . . .
    (refer to your interests and ideas)

4.  As a result I would be able to . . .
    (say what advantages it would bring)

## PROFILE POSTSCRIPT

You have now had the chance to review your work autobiography
and to complete your personal and career profile, consisting of
descriptions of your:

- achievements
- values
- work interests
- work priorities: time and place
- significant influences
- career fantasy

In addition to the self-review questionnaire, there may be other
items you will need to add to your profile. Almost certainly you
will want to reflect on your educational achievements and log the
qualifications you currently hold, and there may well be other
aspects of your personal circumstances that you will need to
include.

The self-assessment summary is a statement about you and your career to date and will reflect the kind of person you are. If you are looking for a complete career change, you may feel it unnecessary to reflect on your previous work experience. After all, you might say, 'I want to make a fresh start and forget the past. I want to do something entirely different.' Chances are, however, that you will carry forward some element of your previously acquired skills and experience, however small, into your new work setting. More importantly, however, it is the process of reflection itself which will be useful in prompting you to think about your future and in making decisions about your next steps. Your personal reflection on your career to date is an essential component of the career planning cycle. The product, your description of your interests, skills and abilities will almost certainly be useful for the process of job search when promoting yourself to potential employers.

# Chapter Four

# What Your Employer Can Do For You

*An organization is neither conscious nor alive. Its value is instrumental and derivative. It is not good in itself; it is good only to the extent that it promotes the good of the individuals who are the parts of the collective whole.*

Aldous Huxley, *Brave New World Revisited*

For those of us in work there is often the hope or expectation that our career will 'progress' with our present employer and that in return for our effort and commitment there may be some reward in terms of increased pay or promotion or, at least, the opportunity to review our career progression at regular intervals. This expectation may be increasingly unrealistic for all the reasons outlined earlier, but the idea of career progression within an organization is firmly rooted in the public consciousness. Indeed, some employing organizations have in the past made a major commitment to the career development of their employees. Large organizations, across all business sectors, have been able to offer centrally organized career progression, particularly for management staff. Very often the employers concerned have espoused a 'home grown' approach to meeting their management manpower needs by developing their own staff. At career entry points, too, employees may have a clearly defined training and development programme lasting two or more years. The graduate chartered accountancy trainee will have a training contract giving precise details of the training and development they can expect. Graduate engineers embarking on a company training scheme leading to chartered engineer status will similarly have a clearly defined plan of training and work experience.

It is important to acknowledge, however, that many of the career management programmes for managers and new professional entrants are not necessarily introduced out of benevolence or a concern for individual needs, but for the strategic good of the employer – to ensure succession planning and to retain a high quality staff in order to keep the organization sufficiently competitive in business terms. According to Handy (1985), attempts to provide centrally-managed career programmes for managers have their own particular emphasis, being concerned to develop 'the best' rather than finding a suitable niche in the organization for every individual, so that 'career development becomes a human hurdle race, the hurdles being different appointments at different levels of authority. He who clears a hurdle can progress to the next, until there are no more.' This sort of system meets the organization's objectives, ensuring at face value the survival of the fittest.

## THE PSYCHOLOGICAL CONTRACT

For most of us selected to perform a specific job, however, the training and development commitment can be very limited. We may have some form of induction or initial training, but that is all. And yet we still have expectations that the employing organization will take into account our needs and aspirations. We need to feel that our work is appreciated; that our efforts are rewarded and that our self-esteem is upheld and our motivation maintained. We might expect promotion or advancement. This expectation on the part of the employee is seen increasingly as part of the psychological contract, which, according to Schein (1978), represents a set of unwritten mutual expectations – what the employee expects to give to and receive from the organization, and what the organization expects to give to and realize from the employee.

How organizations handle the management of employees' expectations and how they respond to the aspirations of individual workers is seen to be distinct from the contract of employment which lays down the financial and legal entitlement of employees. The psychological contract is unwritten, largely, and it takes a very astute job seeker to assess exactly what kind of commitment a potential employer might make to the development of its employees. For those in work, a useful exercise is to answer the following checklist of questions to identify the extent of your organization's commitment to training and development, and to begin to define the psychological contract you have with your own employer, particularly in relation to your personal and career development.

- Does your employer have a policy for the personal and career development of its employees?

- Do you have frequent appraisal interviews? If so, do they have a development focus?

- Do you have access to training or development activities on a regular basis?

- Is there financial support for your training – course fees? day release? Is this well publicized?

- Are the specific activities or events designed to assist your career development?

- Are you routinely consulted about your training and development needs?

If you are unable to answer 'yes' to some of these questions you are not alone. Most attitude surveys of employees and their career development suggest that they have little say in the way their career develops and that their employer contributes little to the process. In one survey of managers and professionals aged 40–55 (Lewis and McLaverty, 1991), 45 per cent had received no career development in the last 5 years; 85 per cent stated clear aspirations and development needs. Some 27 per cent, however, claimed to have access to careers advice. These findings, like many others, suggest that many people in the workplace have development needs, but that these needs are only partially met, if at all. And while they may have the opportunity to discuss their career ideas, organizations do not regularly provide career development opportunities for their staff.

## WHY SHOULD YOUR EMPLOYER BE CONCERNED WITH YOUR CAREER DEVELOPMENT?

The changes in the size and shape of employing organizations outlined in Chapter 1 have provided employers, both public and private, with a range of personnel and human resource problems. Firstly, how can they offer upward career progression when there are fewer tiers of management? Secondly, how can they shift staff from technologically redundant processes and functions? Thirdly, how can they maintain motivation when fewer opportunities exist for career development? In response to these pressing human resource management problems, many employers have had to invest in ways of helping employees cope with changed prospects, and of managing employee expectations. The aim of this chapter is to highlight the range of initiatives that employers can offer, if senior managers have the foresight and commitment to introduce them.

Organizations vary tremendously in their attitudes to their workforce and its needs. Employers with an avowed 'hire and fire' culture are hardly likely to make a serious commitment to employee career development, and while it may be appropriate for Japanese or German companies to enter into a form of social contract with employees – job security in return for loyalty and productivity – many UK employers have been content to shed labour at the first hint of recession rather than retrain, reskill or redeploy employees. At the same time, public sector organizations have been less able to make any commitment to employee career development, constrained by public expenditure cuts and policy changes affecting the nature of service organizations. It is, however, clear that many employing organizations have begun to take career management seriously in the face of the revised employment scenario outlined earlier, and for the following reasons:

- to retain their 'best' staff or those with particular skills and expertise – core workers in key positions;

- to encourage flexibility by equipping staff to handle change and enable 'multi-skilling';

- to manage careers in new ways, encouraging staff to become more 'self-managing' in their career development;

- to achieve gains in motivation and productivity at a time when opportunities for promotion and conventional career progression are limited.

What follows is a brief summary of the range of career management initiatives that some employees can expect from their employers and an analysis of the way they can support the process of career development. Many are comparatively recent in origin and still subject to piloting and evaluation. Most have been instigated for one or more of the reasons outlined above, but all have the effect of drawing attention to career issues and aim to support individual employees in their career development. There is, however, no universally agreed solution. Employers have adopted different approaches in their career management practices. The BBC, for example, has invested in career resource centres which employees can visit to find out information about opportunities both inside and outside the Corporation. ICI, by contrast, uses workshops and portfolios. Many organizations now have 'career development managers' or particular staff charged with the delivery of a set of career management activities. The range of activities described below is designed to be illustrative of the kind of support you could in future expect from an employer.

## APPRAISAL INTERVIEWS

When you want to talk about your career, much of the support you might find will occur on an informal and spontaneous basis, by talking to colleagues, managers and personnel staff. In most organizations, however, formal appraisal systems exist which can offer the opportunity to assess your past performance, identify your training and development needs and future potential. Inevitably, therefore, the appraisal interview is seen as an essential ingredient in the career management process giving, as it can, personal feedback which assists self-appraisal and the chance to review options for personal and career development. For the employer, it is seen as the natural link between the goals of the organization and the aspirations of individuals within it.

However, the potential of the appraisal process for career planning can be limited by a number of factors. Firstly, the appraisal may be more concerned with an assessment of past performance than setting an agenda for future development. Secondly, discussion of training and development needs may reflect the demands of the immediate job, and the broader development needs and goals of the individual may not be adequately addressed. At the same time, the appraisal process assumes that managers are both trained and skilled in this form of interviewing, which they may not be. For it to be successful, appraisal assumes a climate of openness and trust.

At best, the appraisal interview, skillfully handled, can provide an opportunity for an open and honest discussion about individual development needs enabling the appraisee to feel both valued and rewarded. At worst, it can be characterized by a complete lack of openness and trust and reflect serious problems in the workplace culture. Some employees feel threatened by the process, others invest very little of themselves in the activity. As one employee put it:

> *In my department, appraisal is designed to bring staff into line, to get staff to do more than they are already doing. It's not about your own development, the managers are trying to get you to do what they want. There's a risk that you agree to do things you don't want to do, to do extra.*
>
> *My advice is to go with prepared answers to the likely questions and not say anything you haven't already thought about. Above all, don't sign any written summary immediately – take your time to think about the implications.*

The cynicism may not just rest with the appraised. As one manager put it, 'it's the usual story – boasts, moans and a wish list.' In situations such as the one described, it is difficult to see the relevance of appraisal to the process of career planning, which requires openness and honesty in reviewing hopes and aspirations for the future. According to Handy (1985), the procedure is often ineffective because the manager or workplace supervisor is expected to be both judge and counsellor, which leads to role conflict. For Fletcher and Williams (1985), too much is simply expected of the process.

> *'The typical appraisal system is trying to do too much with too little; the wonder is that it manages to do as well as it does.'*

Given these apparent limitations, it is understandable that other means of addressing career issues represent a more profitable line of approach and put the discussion about individual development in a broader context, setting it apart from on-the-job performance and the relationship between manager and managed.

## PERSONAL AND CAREER DEVELOPMENT PORTFOLIOS

A recent innovation, offered as yet by comparatively few employers, portfolios provide employees with a written record of their personal and career development and at the same time point to the range of job opportunities which exist within the employing organization. In one sense, this book is a form of portfolio, enabling you to reflect on your experience to date, appraise your abilities and achievements and make plans for the future. All portfolios are designed to support these processes. How are they used? Where portfolios have been introduced by employers, they show a number of common characteristics. Portfolios are:

- provided by the employer but owned by the employee and used voluntarily to set plans for personal and career development
- based on the same process of self-appraisal encouraged by this book
- used either in conjunction with the appraisal process, so that the line manager is required to review, and take seriously, the aspirations of the employee, or as a basis for a discussion with a mentor
- often designed to include sample job descriptions and person specifications to illustrate the range of possible jobs within the organization.

What are the benefits for the users? Employers introducing portfolios for the first time have done so for a variety of reasons, but their main motive has been to encourage individuals to take greater responsibility for their own development. They are also important in charting the employee's progress to professional status and continuing professional development. Indeed, the Engineering Council's career management portfolio was intended for use by graduate engineers *en route* to Chartered status, with graduates invited to record their progress and experience.

In order to be successful, portfolios rely on the willingness of employees to complete them and take them seriously. As with most self-help materials, the format, design and written style are of paramount importance. They therefore require considerable evaluation effort during their preparation. At the same time portfolios, it has to be acknowledged, may not work for everyone and many people will prefer some form of human interaction when exploring their ideas, and reviewing their experience. Nevertheless, they provide a portable and easy to use framework for some of the fundamental career planning processes, and from the employer's perspective they can be introduced at a comparatively low cost.

## COMPUTER-ASSISTED CAREER GUIDANCE SYSTEMS

Another form of self-help activity, CACG systems can provide employees with considerable help in the processes of self-appraisal.

A number of software products have been designed for use in employment settings and are readily available. Some employers are increasingly using these alongside databases profiling jobs which exist both inside and outside the organization. This enables users to match their own profiles of skills and job interests with concrete career opportunities which exist elsewhere. The benefits of using CACG systems in their various forms are described in more detail in Chapter 2.

## CAREER PLANNING AND CAREER DEVELOPMENT WORKSHOPS

Career workshops, while not widely offered by employers, are becoming seen as an increasingly effective way of managing career aspirations and encouraging employees to take greater control over their career development. They are particularly appropriate in organizations which are about to face major change and reorganization; helping employees to cope with aspirations which may not be being met, or assisting with the life-stage transitions of those in the workplace. In terms of content, they embody many of the elements and processes of career planning. Typical activities might include, for example:

- life and work experience review
- self-appraisal of personal skills, values, interests
- defining options for change
- setting personal goals
- planning a course of action.

They offer participants an opportunity to review their personal and career development in a non-competitive, usually stress-free and supportive environment, making considerable use of questionnaire and other written stimulus material. Their style will largely be determined by the skills of the workshop facilitator(s), but in the main these are highly participative events, relying on a certain amount of self-disclosure and the use of participants as peer counsellors. Their length, precise structure and availability will vary considerably, but in contrast to the assessment centres mentioned earlier, the outcomes of these events are usually confidential to the group and individual participants. The results are not intended for the employer or senior managers in the organization.

From the perspective of you, the participant, what are the

advantages? Typically, there will be three outcomes in particular for participants, which make the experience of taking part in a career workshop both rewarding and enjoyable.

Firstly, the personal review process, coupled with the opportunity to reflect on one's life achievements, invariably increases one's sense of self-worth and self-confidence, particularly if your hopes and aspirations are shared with other career changers in a mutually supportive environment.

Secondly, a career workshop is an ideal venue to bring to the fore ideas for your future that have either been submerged for a long time, or that you have thought about but not expressed openly. Participating in a workshop can therefore allow you to take a creative view of your future career, to generate fresh ideas for your development.

Thirdly, the emphasis on self-appraisal and personal review is likely to result in some new self-insight or awareness. For example, what you may consider a personal failure on your part may in the eyes of other people be both understandable and the result of factors beyond your control. Experience that you may see as limited and inconsequential may on closer inspection be far more important than you first thought. The potential benefits for those who take part can, therefore, be considerable.

From the employer's point of view, career planning workshops are comparatively expensive in terms of staff time. Typically, they can accommodate about a dozen participants and last for one or two days. The fear for employers, of course, is that employees taking part will be more inclined to make a job move and leave the organization once they have had the chance to clarify their career plans. Research cited by Jackson (1990) of the Institute for Employment Studies, however, suggests that this is not necessarily the case, with the majority of participants implementing changes to their current job and undertaking company training. Nevertheless, 29 per cent of participants in the same employer study identified implementing job changes as an outcome of the workshop. Others reported changes in long-term career aims and in their personal lives as a result of workshop participation.

Participants in career planning workshops are almost certainly going to make some kind of change to their work or personal lives. 'No change' is an outcome that is unlikely to be reported. The final stage of the workshop, in which participants are encouraged to set goals and define their plan of action, is frequently a public process in which individual intentions are affirmed by other members of the group. This invariably commits participants to carry out the aims and objectives they set for themselves. And, indeed, it is perfectly possible to use other members of the group to support you in carrying out your plans once the workshop is over.

From the individual's point of view, career workshops, properly facilitated, offer a very positive experience and provide considerable impetus for career change. They need not, of course, be run by an employer. A number of organizations provide this kind of event, particularly women's organizations. Once you have participated in and rehearsed the processes involved, it becomes much easier to move through the career planning process for yourself. One part of the process that workshops do not usually include is that of research. Their emphasis will be on personal review and action planning. If you participate, you are likely to have to carry out a considerable amount of further work to put your ideas into practice; to research the opportunities that are available to you.

## MENTORS AND MENTORING

Many of us can point to one or two key people who have been helpful to us in our careers to date, either by offering support, providing ideas and suggestions or acting as a role model for our own development. We may not have thought of these people as mentors, but they may have performed this function, albeit on an informal level, by influencing our thoughts and ideas, or shaping our experience.

What is mentoring? Simply stated, mentoring describes a relationship in which another more experienced individual helps to guide someone who is less experienced. Very often mentoring schemes are provided for new employees or recent entrants to a particular profession, to assist with the processes of transition to a new working environment. Mentoring need not, however, be limited to situations in which the 'old hand' guides the 'novice' worker. There is no reason at all why mentoring should not take place between those of equal experience or status, or indeed at any career stage.

What can mentors offer? According to Kram (1986), research studies have shown that mentoring can help on both 'career' issues and 'psychosocial' functions. On the one hand, mentors can act as sponsors, promoting the interests of individual protégés in the employing organization, coaching them so that they adopt the right strategies for career advancement, and generally ensuring that they gain an appropriate mix of experience and exposure in their employing organization. On the other hand, mentors can offer counselling, acceptance and friendship and at the same time offer themselves as role models to their protégés, who will be able to gain a clearer sense of their own development needs as a result of the mentoring relationship.

What form of help? In practice, mentors can offer a wide range of assistance in the process of maintaining and developing your career. These include:

* advice on strategy and tactics in career development
* information about opportunities available for change or advancement either with your present employer or elsewhere
* personal contacts who can be useful for further help
* an insider view of organizational culture, and, particularly, likely changes which will impact on jobs
* a sounding-board for your ideas for the future.

These helping processes need not, of course, be the sole preserve of people who are formally called 'mentors'. We may rely on a wide network of personal support – including family and friends – to inform and counsel us in our career development. Support groups can be particularly effective in promoting equal opportunity issues. Membership of a professional association may well offer the opportunity of peer support as well as 'mentoring' in its classic sense.

If your employer has a formally assigned mentoring programme, it is likely that several criteria will have to be observed if the programme is to work effectively, according to Jackson (1993):

* The relationship between mentor and protégé must be confidential. It is for this reason that many mentor programmes do not involve an individual and their line manager, but rely on staff across the organization.
* Mentors should be willing to participate voluntarily.
* Both mentors and protégés need training in making the mentoring relationship work.
* Programmes have to be flexible enough to allow for individual differences. Not everyone needs a mentor, and those who do may need to change their mentor if the relationship fails.

With these caveats, it is clear from the research to date that mentor schemes can produce positive outcomes for the participants. One study by Fagenson (1989) found that mentored individuals reported having more career mobility or opportunity for change, recognition, satisfaction and promotion than non-mentored individuals. Further research will be required to see if mentoring schemes can succeed on one important criterion – that of encouraging personal ownership of career issues, rather than creating a form of dependency. If, as may be the case, mentoring is not formally adopted in your organization, it will be worthwhile to look around you to see who might be able to help you in this way. It's quite likely that whoever you approach will be flattered by your request!

## THE CAREER MANAGEMENT MIX

Most of the employer initiatives mentioned in this chapter are designed to encourage greater autonomy on the part of individual employees and are part of a matrix of career initiatives, as the profile below illustrates.

---

**Employer Profile : The BBC**

In its policy on staff development, the BBC clearly equates career development not with promotion but with 'growth for the individual, i.e. the acquisition of new skills, the development of existing ones, new knowledge and increased inter-personal effectiveness.'

To this end, it has established a number of resource centres or Careerpoints which staff can use on a self-referral basis to review their career progress and research options for futher development. The centres provide:

- career information resources
- computer-assisted guidance systems
- career planning materials

Much of the initial career management effort was spent on running career development workshops for different staff. While these were seen as successful, new initiatives were needed to link the issue of 'career' more closely with the systems of appraisal and staff training, and as a result, the main focus in future will be on the use of Open Learning Workbooks to assist individual staff in their career development.

---

In addition to the activities and resources described above, there are several steps that employers can take to increase their commitment to employees and their career aspirations. They can, for example:

- provide a 'career working group' to act as a focus for career management and to improve communication to staff

- ensure that job vacancies are advertised internally with detailed job descriptions and skills specifications

- develop 'job maps' to illustrate particular career paths in the organization, or career routes that have been taken by particular employees

- offer planned secondments or exchanges of staff between functions as a form of development activity

- research staff development needs and aspirations on a regular, organization-wide basis.

A key concern here must be to give more and widely available information to all staff about the organization and the jobs within it. As one personnel and training specialist put it, 'we give more information to the stockbrokers in the City than we do to our own employees'.

At a broader level still, there are many ways in which employers can facilitate the career development of staff, particularly female staff. The adoption of 'family-friendly' policies, the use of workplace nurseries, career break schemes and, above all, a commitment to equal opportunities policies can have a marked effect on the organizational culture and increase the range of options of those committed to their career development, but at the same time wanting to manage the competing demands of family and workplace. We ought to be able to look forward to a time when the majority of employers offer a range of provision, a matrix of policies and interventions designed to facilitate the career development of individual employees.

Any employing organization wishing to promote 'career' and to manage the career development of its employees is, as we have seen, faced with a number of dilemmas. The first is to be able to provide career-focused activities for a wide range of employees at comparatively low cost, and therefore be clear about the potential of the different interventions described above. Secondly, the employer may need to acknowledge that individual employees will

---

**Job sharing: Gloucestershire County Council**

---

Job sharing was introduced in 1988, with the aim, from the employee perspective, of improving the career development of part-timers, enhancing access for women to senior management and enabling existing staff to reduce working time. From the organization's perspective the gains were seen in terms of reduced levels of absence, increased productivity and in attracting high quality staff.

All posts are eligible to be job-shared unless a department's chief officer decides otherwise. Thus far, there are 118 job sharers out of the total employee count of 12,800. Few, however, are in senior posts.

In creating job shares, working patterns are left to the discretion of line managers, but each partner receives an individual contract of employment. Where job tasks are divided, a job description addendum specifies the tasks to be done. Conditions of service are applied on a pro rata basis.

As a result of early operating problems of the scheme, a new code of practice on opportunities for flexible learning has been drawn up for managers.

(Source: Job Sharing: Incomes Data Services,
Study 548, February 1994.)

---

differ widely in their needs and aspirations. One person's fulfilment is another person's boredom, and not all staff will show the same enthusiasm for 'development' whatever its guise.

Finally, given the difficulties (outlined in Chapter 1) faced by employers in making a commitment to the long-term career development of their employees, and the expectation of most workers that a 'career' will be characterized by career advancement, employers are left with two related options. On the one hand, they can offer opportunities for personal rather than career development, giving employees an increased range of education, training and other forms of development activity. This effectively removes the onus of providing career development for employees, and more positively it creates a better trained, motivated and intentionally more flexible workforce. On the other hand, they can offer employability rather than planned career development. This implies a commitment to the training and development of individual workers, by offering a range of workplace experience and skill enhancement which ensures employees' continued employment with their present employer, and also offers greater marketability in the wider job market should employees need to look elsewhere for work. Different groups of professionals have come to expect this revision of the psychological contract, but its wider extension to all employees now seems possible. One clear implication of this changed scenario is that individuals are expected to take greater control over, and manage, their own career development, but that they are entitled to an increased level of support from their employers in doing so. As Mayo (1992) points out, career development is increasingly seen as a legitimate concern for all employees but in future this will not imply increased status or promotion. Rather, career development will be concerned with increasing the personal value of those at work, by a continuous commitment to growth and learning.

# Chapter Five

# You and Your Development

*Somewhere along the line of development we discover what we really are, and then we make our real decision for which we are responsible. Make that decision primarily for yourself because you can never really live anyone else's life, not even your own child's. The influence you exert is through your own life and what you become yourself.*
Eleanor Roosevelt, quoted in
*Eleanor and Franklin* by Joseph P. Lash

Personal development can take many different forms. You might want to gain particular skills or increase your knowledge. You may want to gain a higher qualification to compete more effectively in the job market. Alternatively, you could simply want to invest more time in yourself by developing your self-understanding and insight, becoming more creative, or giving expression to some long-suppressed personal interest. The main emphasis of the present chapter is not a prescription for life-long personal development, but to show how different forms of development activity can help meet your career objectives.

Given the uncertainty in the world of work, outlined earlier, we need to invest more of our time in learning and development, both to anticipate future change in the work environment and to help us cope, at an individual level, with the effects of change. Engaging in development activity can assist us to acquire new skills to help us survive in a competitive job market and may prevent or remedy the increasing amount of strain we are subject to. At the same time, our investment in personal development is now a life-long process. The early-retired are as likely to engage in educational programmes as those in younger age groups. As Watts (1993) points out, forms of education and training are no longer simply a preparation for adult life, but are now seen as a vital element throughout working life. Our commitment to personal development needs now to be ongoing and continuous.

What appear to be emerging, however, are two distinct forms of personal development. On the one hand, there is the notion of development as personal growth and learning in whatever context. Voluntary work overseas, completing a degree course for the intellectual challenge, or taking part in a sporting or creative activity, all provide opportunities for personal development which may help us grow as individuals by exposing us to challenge and offering us fresh insight into our values and personality.

By contrast, a more task-centred and competency model of personal development is being increasingly advanced by employing organizations. Unable to offer employees opportunities for career progression and advancement, some organizations offer training opportunities to maintain staff motivation. In return, they expect a benefit from this kind of investment in terms of increased productivity and flexibility on the employees' part. To some extent, this instrumental view of development has emerged from management development processes, but is now being extended to a wider cross-section of the workforce. Typically, employer-based development planning is characterized by one or more of the following objectives:

- to identify individual training needs, very often as part of the appraisal process

- to encourage development within the job as well as for lateral career moves

- to help employees gain professional accreditation

- to make individual staff more responsible for their own personal and career development by encouraging ownership of their working futures

- to review employees' core competencies for their level of work and identify specific development objectives on a year-by-year basis.

In some organizations, such development programmes are voluntary, in others compulsory, and clearly this kind of job-related development is a far cry from the person-centred growth model referred to earlier, and raises key questions about the owner of such programmes – the employer or the employee? This is in marked contrast to the non-career focused personal growth model described above.

## YOUR DEVELOPMENT NEEDS

What are your own development needs? Are you looking for a general sense of direction and purpose? Do you want to make a change in your life? Do you need more confidence in dealing with clients, or managing other staff? Or are there specific skills you would like to develop, such as writing research proposals or managing meetings? Try to describe how you might improve your situation in answering one or more of the questions below:

What kind of improvements you would like to make in your life and work?

Which skills do you want or feel you need to develop?

Which additional qualifications you would like to gain?

When you review the development needs you have described you may be able to gain a clearer view of your motives. Those leaving education, particularly, may well have a career goal in mind and need additional training in order to achieve it. What potential employers may see as a lack of qualifications and skills, needs to be made good. Yours may be an instrumental view in which personal development may be a means to an end, such as getting a better job.

Those in early to mid-career may be bored with their present work and life and need a new stimulus. If you are in this situation you may want further development and perhaps a chance to opt out of the job market for a while in order to 'stretch yourself' and increase your self-esteem. You may know intuitively how you would like to develop, often without thought of any pay-off in terms of career change or progression. You are concerned primarily with personal growth.

As a result of the changes in the job market outlined in Chapter 1, and the stress and uncertainty evoked by them, there may also be a far more strategic motive for personal development, with a far sharper focus. If you are in employment and you are fearful of job security, personal development may well be defined by your ability to maintain your position in the face of increased change and competition. You may well be asking the following questions:

- What kind of people and skills will my employing organization need?

- What value does it place on my contribution? How can I help meet its future needs?

In this scenario, decisions about your personal development may well be instrumental, but the focus is clearly on meeting organizational needs rather than your own.

Finally, for professionals of all kinds – freelancers, the self-employed, and employees – there is a clear need to maintain one's credibility in the eyes of clients or potential employers. By keeping in touch with the latest developments in your work, you can both improve your work performance and increase your value in the labour market. This is particularly important in fast developing business areas such as information technology, or work frequently affected by legislation or where there is a regular influx of new ideas and innovative practice, such as management training and development. The need for professional updating is yet another motive for taking part in development activity.

## A KEY TO YOUR DEVELOPMENT NEEDS

If you are leaving education and looking for work for the first time, you may feel that your development needs have been met. Your priority is work experience. For most people in this situation, however, further training is inevitable and the new venue will be the workplace. Graduates from vocational courses will be encouraged to qualify for professional status. Those from non-vocational programmes may well need further full- or part-time training for a particular job. Or alternatively they may use a 'stepping-stone' approach and accumulate a range of experience with different employers. Whatever the career pattern, the process of developing skills and increasing knowledge goes on unabated.

To assist with this period of transition from education to work and to anticipate your future development needs, one key process will help – identifying your personal skills and qualities. You may have already completed the skills questionnaire in Chapter 3, but try to take it several stages further. Reflecting on your own educational experience, try to list the skills and knowledge you have gained. This could be associated with course content, e.g. knowledge of foreign languages or computer software, but also with the teaching and learning methods you experienced, e.g. team working or carrying out library research. Next, try to analyse the skill demands of the work you may be doing. As a result you will be able to see the transferability of your skills from one setting to another, and set an agenda for your future development. In addition it will help you value the skills and qualities you have to offer, and those that you are about to use. And if, as is sometimes the case, the kind of work you choose fails to match your expectations, the time spent on this process will almost certainly help you in choosing another type of work.

For those presently at work, a useful indicator of your development needs is the degree of satisfaction you obtain from your present job or work role. You may be dissatisfied with your current situation and feel that to give yourself the extra confidence to move on you need further training or an additional qualification. By contrast, you may be reasonably happy in your current work, but feel that you need to invest time in your development to anticipate future job changes. Whatever the reason, it is important both to review your present situation and to assess the potential of different kinds of development for meeting your needs. This is often a great deal easier than it sounds. Faced with a variety of issues – performing effectively, balancing work and home life, satisfying your own interests – it is often difficult to recognize your real needs and set priorities in meeting them. And if the employing organization is changing around you, it is often difficult to see when a fundamental mismatch occurs between you and the culture of the workplace, as the following case illustrates:

## ❏ Case Study: Andrea
*Andrea graduated in psychology and spent several years specializing in human resource management. After that, she decided to work in a consultancy using her knowledge and previous experience. After a short*

*time, however, the work became less rewarding and more stressful for a variety of reasons. Having children meant that she was more family-centred; parenting was overriding her commitment to her career and the job appeared to be making too many demands on her home life because it involved travel away from her work base.*

*At the same time a change of management brought her a new boss who seemed to have expectations that Andrea couldn't meet. Increasingly she felt that there was a lack of fit between her style and the new organizational culture that was emerging. Her values had changed in one direction and the other staff seemed to be heading in another direction entirely. Not only was her job not in tune with her personal values, it was not using what she now saw as her core skills, the interpersonal and team working skills common to many of the helping professions. In short, she needed work which was more person-centred.*

A number of themes occur in Andrea's account which are common to many people in various stages of their career – the need to balance home life and work life; the inevitable tensions between the expectations of managers and the wishes of their staff; the goodness of 'fit' between the needs of the organization's individual workers and the culture of the larger working group. In Holland's terms, Andrea's 'social type' no longer fitted the emerging 'enterprising' environment provided by the employer (Holland, 1966). Her wish to change her work was also prompting a review of her development needs.

## MOTIVES FOR CHANGE AND DEVELOPMENT

If you are feeling dissatisfied with your current work situation, it is important to recognize why that is so before making development plans. At least one major study (Dyer, 1983) showed that there are a number of frequently cited reasons for dissatisfaction among employees. Of these, the most highly ranked were as follows:

- Lack of opportunity for reward and growth in one's job:
  On the one hand, employees are concerned about the fairness of systems of promotion and the apparent lack of relationship between good performance and career progression. On the other, they want greater access to training in order to further their career development.

- Lack of challenge or excitement in one's job:
  People want opportunities for job enrichment to be able to develop in their work and bring their skills and competencies into play.

- Lack of understanding of, and commitment to, the organization's goals:
  Employees naturally want to feel that their work contributes to the success of the organization, but many are unable to make this connection.

- Lack of information about oneself and the organization:
  People want to know what is happening in their organization – about new job opportunities, and feedback about their performance. They need communication and dialogue at all levels within the organization.

- Crisis management:
  Employees bemoan the lack of long-range planning and complain that so much change is simply a response to an immediate crisis.

Clearly, many of the respondents to this survey were concerned about their personal and career development and felt that their employers could have done more in this domain. What of your own experience? Completing the following short questionnaire may help you assess the degree of satisfaction you have in your current work. It may help you to single out particular issues which you need to work on, or gauge your overall level of satisfaction. Simply rate each of the statements in the questionnaire:

## YOUR WORK SATISFACTION

Please circle one of the numbers against each statement:

|  | Agree |  |  | Disagree |  |
|---|---|---|---|---|---|
| I feel relatively successful in what I do | 5 | 4 | 3 | 2 | 1 |
| On balance, my work is satisfying | 5 | 4 | 3 | 2 | 1 |
| I can use my skills to good effect | 5 | 4 | 3 | 2 | 1 |
| I have access to training and development | 5 | 4 | 3 | 2 | 1 |
| I feel positive about my career prospects | 5 | 4 | 3 | 2 | 1 |
| I don't feel valued at work | 1 | 2 | 3 | 4 | 5 |
| I'd like more reward from my work | 1 | 2 | 3 | 4 | 5 |
| There is little opportunity to discuss my career plans | 1 | 2 | 3 | 4 | 5 |
| I feel that I've outgrown my job | 1 | 2 | 3 | 4 | 5 |
| I often wish I could change career direction | 1 | 2 | 3 | 4 | 5 |

When you have rated each of the statements, add the scores together to arrive at your total. Then review your current level of job satisfaction below:

**Over 40**
You seem quite happy with your current lot, but this is not necessarily an excuse for inaction. You will still have to identify your development needs in order to maintain your level of motivation. Are there changes on the horizon that you need to anticipate in your work or personal life, for instance?

**Between 20 and 40**
Your satisfaction with work could obviously be improved. Are there particular issues which need your attention? Do you need a greater level of reward for what you do? Are you stagnating because of a lack of challenge? Are your skills not being tapped? When you have identified the primary issues you can take action which may remedy the situation. The development case studies which follow may provide you with some useful ideas.

**20 and below**
Depending on how you feel, you may need to take some urgent steps in order to avoid any feeling of work stress or burnout. This may well involve a major effort on your part to tell other people around you about your situation. Your line manager should be aware of your feelings as a result of your regular appraisal. If this is not appropriate, you may need to find a mentor figure who can help, or other people in the organization who can support you. Almost certainly you will benefit from professional careers counselling to explore your options for development and change.

## REVIEWING YOUR PSYCHOLOGICAL CONTRACT

Now that you have assessed your degree of work satisfaction, it is useful to go one step further. As we saw earlier, we all have expectations about the way our employer might respond to our needs for personal and career development. This unwritten psychological contract is reflected in our attitude to work and is centred on our initial expectations about pay, progression and the way our performance is appraised. But as Schein (1978) points out, the contract is constantly being renegotiated in the light of experience. What is the nature of the psychological contract you have with your employer? The following questions should help you review your expectations about your work in order to pinpoint those which you feel have not been met, and also to highlight any positive outcomes:

- How were you hoping your career would progress? To stay in the same job? To gain rapid promotion? To develop workplace skills?

- In practice, what has been your experience? How were your expectations met, if at all?

- What opportunities have there been to make your development needs known to your employer?

- How far have these needs been met?

- What opportunities, if any, exist for your personal and career development with your present employer?

- What career path might your line manager and colleagues envisage for you?

- What has been the experience of people who have moved on from your kind of job? Are there examples of successful progressions within the organization or outside it?

On the basis of your answers to these questions you may be able to decide on appropriate action and perhaps redefine the contract you have with your employer. Defining your development needs and trying to meet them, with or without your employer's help, can be an important first step. You might want to make your line manager aware of your ideas, or contact the training or human resource staff to see what kind of development opportunities exist. If you sense that what you need most is a change, it will be helpful to discuss your development needs with a professional careers counsellor.

Decisions of this kind are, however, seldom taken in isolation from other life events for those in early to mid-career. Finance for further full-time study, for example, may only be possible if you have the financial support of a partner or if you are able to find suitable crèche facilities for pre-school children. Even attending short residential courses can prove problematic in terms of child care. The notion of life stage is therefore an important factor in discussing career change and personal development.

## LIFE STAGE AND CAREER CHANGE

For those in mid-life, the process of career change is often made more complex by the sheer range of factors which need to be taken into account. Often choices and decisions will need to reflect the wishes of partners, take into account the location of family and friends, and acknowledge the impact of change on other people. Career decisions at this point become a question of balancing several competing forces, rather than a straightforward decision about the suitability of a particular kind of work.

At the same time, the motivation to change career direction may be a response to changing values or interests. The freelance editor who suddenly finds her work routine and dull may wish to change direction, but the main problem will be to identify in which direction her values and needs are leading. Those faced with redundancy, the onset of poor health or disability or changed personal circumstances will be faced with similar questions. Very often, therefore, those in mid-career will need to trade off one aim or desire against another, rather than work for optimum solutions to the 'career question'. This process is summarized by Ginzberg, (1972):

> While I still believe that few individuals make occupational choices that satisfy all of their principal needs and desires, I now think that a more

*correct formulation is that of* optimization. *Men and women seek to find the best occupational fit between their changing desires and their changing circumstances. This search is a continuing one. As long as they entertain the possibility of shifting their goals, they are constantly considering a new balance in which the potential gains are weighed against the probable costs.*

According to life stage theorists, this process may also reflect the changing concerns of those at different life stages. It was Levinson's (1978) research which provided an analysis of life stage in terms of career and personal relationships. On the basis of his research, Levinson argues that people pass through several predictable age-related stages during their lives and that the major life transitions each take several years to accomplish. The stages are outlined in Table 5.1.

According to Levinson, men (his research focused on men's career development) in the mid-life transition often changed their personal priorities by spending more time with their family and reducing the amount of their lives devoted to work. It was often a time when individuals embarked on a second career, having reappraised their career direction and embarked on a process of greater 'individualization' to become more their own person, to achieve a fuller sense of their own individuality.

The need for change and development may therefore be a feature of a particular stage of life. The mid-life transition is a period of moderate or even severe crisis in which every aspect of someone's life comes into question. This 'radical critique' centres on all aspects of life, including career, and can take the form of a restless review of one's direction and purpose. It is important, therefore, to be able to recognize the symptoms of the mid-life crisis in setting a development agenda. Various kinds of development activity will help test out new ideas, or revisit ideas that have previously been discarded, and help to counter feelings of frustration and, possibly, failure.

The periods of transition have obvious significance for the processes of career review and career planning. In these, especially in the early adult phase, individuals will be imagining alternative career options, reassessing themselves and their personal priorities in much the same way as people making initial career choices. The tasks and skills of career planning are, therefore, just as appropriate in mid-career as they are for 'early adults'.

In reviewing life stage theory, however, it is perhaps worth

*Table 5.1:* Levinson's developmental periods of early and middle adulthood

| | |
|---|---|
| **Age 17-22** | Early adult transition:<br>A period of increasing independence in the adult world. |
| **Mid-Twenties** | Becoming increasingly autonomous and established. |
| **Age 28–33** | Age 30 transition:<br>Often characterized by a questioning of life direction which may involve career change. For some, a period of confusion and turmoil. |
| **Mid-Thirties to early Forties** | A time of creating order and stability, of making deeper commitments in terms of relationships. Levinson calls this 'Becoming one's own man'. |
| **Age 40–45** | The Mid-Life Transition:<br>Levinson sees this period as a bridge between early to middle adulthood. Again, a period of self-doubt, in which there is a yearning to express one's talents and aspirations – 'for the majority of men this is a period of great struggle between the self and the external world'. |
| **Age 45-55** | Age 50 transition:<br>Characterized by similar experiences to the age 30 transition. |
| **Age 55-60** | A period of stability followed in the early sixties by the transition into late adulthood. |

noting that developmental models such as Levinson's are based on life history interviews with American males, who, in the immediate post-war period experienced full employment and high economic growth, and their life histories reflected environmental factors such as these. Any recent study might reveal a very different perspective on life stage and career. A penetrating study by Newman (1993) illustrates the way economic optimism has given way to high unemployment, recession and reduced life choices for the 'baby boom' generation in the United States, pointing to the phenomenon of downward mobility between the generations and very different career expectations and life experiences. Could it be that career patterns and life stages simply reflect a wider economic reality and that in an uncertain future the developmental periods of adult life become rather less predictable?

# DEFINING DEVELOPMENT OPTIONS

Any form of new experience has the power to change your perception of yourself and the world, be it travel to different countries, voluntary work or taking part in an educational programme. This kind of 'development' experience can bring about a range of positive outcomes, enhancing one's self-esteem, perhaps, but also developing fresh insights into oneself and other people. At a simple level, setting oneself new challenges, such as developing interpersonal skills by being in a different social setting, or organizing events for a local club or association is a potent form of self-development. You can gain in self-confidence, become more proactive and even develop particular skills such as time management, planning and organizing. Simply taking part in a one-day programme of activity can bring fresh insight. The following quotations resulted from a one-day experience of work shadowing, designed to help individual students decide on their future career options. For some, there was genuine surprise that they might be acceptable to an employer:

*It was encouraging to find out that the kind of person who makes a successful application to a graduate training scheme was no different to me.*

For others, there was a sense of relief that, at last, they had found a kind of work which would interest them and for which they would be suited:

*I now believe that there is actually a job out there somewhere that I'm suited to, and want to do.*

and also a spur to action:

*I can now see exactly where I need to start and what I need to do now, in order to shape my career.*

While these outcomes resulted from one day of work shadowing, the same potential outcomes can also arise from various forms of informational interviewing and mentoring described in earlier chapters. Talking to other people about their work can be an effective way of shaping your own career goals. Other forms of development activity on a larger scale can have a powerful influence on 'self' and 'career'. What follows is a summary of development options, designed to show their likely outcomes and benefits.

## FURTHER EDUCATION

For those returning to education in the hope of a better job or career change, the first question to ask when making a large investment in your own further education is 'Is it really necessary?' Many people assume that in order to get the job they want, they must have relevant qualifications and training. This may not be the case. The recent graduate with ten years experience in administration, marketing and PR may not need specific training in sales or marketing to return to a similar, more responsible role to the one she left some years before. Very often, relevant experience may count for more than directly relevant training, because you have already demonstrated the competencies required to do the work. Another question to raise when planning further education and training is whether the course and the qualification will lead in the direction that you hope it will. Quite naturally, the first priority of a course provider is to ensure that the course runs. They may be less concerned about whether it is going to meet your precise needs, recognizing that most forms of education and training provide some personal or economic reward. As the 'consumer', there-fore, it is up to you to ensure that the course will open up opportunities rather than narrow them down. There are several ways you can do this. It is perfectly possible to ask to see the employment profile of those who have completed the course previously – what they did next in terms of employment or further education and training. Other measures might include: talking to recent or present students; gaining the perspective of other courses elsewhere; or contacting professional bodies to see what likely membership exemption a course and qualification can offer.

Many students will, of course, be interested in further education as an end in itself. They may want to pursue a particular subject or interest, or experience higher level study for its intellectual challenge. They will be less interested in the instrumental view of further education, and want to study for its own sake rather than as a pathway to a new career.

## THE VOCATIONAL TRAINING OPTION

There are many courses of vocational training at different qualification levels. For career changers and those perhaps with general degrees and non-vocational qualifications, it is important to recognize that many courses offer a 'conversion' to a specific career area and do not necessarily require 'relevant' qualifications for entry. Hence, it is perfectly possible to enter management or computer training with a philosophy degree, or train in journalism with a chemistry background, or for an engineer to undertake social work training. Equally, it is possible to enter engineering training from other backgrounds. The range of development options available may be wider than you imagine and are certainly not limited to the subject of your earlier experience or training. The only likely barrier to entry may be financial – finding sufficient funds to cover the costs of course fees and living costs while retraining.

It is not the aim of the present chapter to give a detailed listing of the kinds of training that are available – there are many course compendia which do this. Rather, its aim is to identify very briefly the types of programme which exist:

### PROFESSIONAL DEVELOPMENT

Many programmes of study are designed for those who are already experienced in a particular career, but want further specialization or a validation of their experience to date. Increasingly the mode and methods of study are geared to those in the workplace, with distance learning materials, such as interactive video, available to offer flexible learning.

### VOCATIONAL TRAINING

Many courses provide direct training in a range of technical and personal skills and at the same time prepare students for direct entry to a particular kind of employment, with the necessary knowledge and preparatory experience. This form of pre-entry training may be offered on both a full- or part-time basis.

### CONVERSION

A particular kind of course exists for those with higher qualifications – that of a conversion course, usually at a post-experience or post-graduate diploma or masters level, enabling you to convert your present qualifications to a qualification which may prepare you for a different career. Courses in computing and IT offer an obvious example.

## FOUNDATION COURSES

Access courses, pre-degree foundation courses in art and design and other subjects, are examples of one-year courses which provide a taster of further education to prepare students for further courses.

Before embarking on a programme of study, it will be useful to research the different modes of study available to you – full-time, part-time, open learning and the degree of flexibility which is possible. Can you, for example, take modules on an occasional basis, rather than complete the course within a given time scale? Will you be given credit for any qualifications you already have? Given the increasing flexibility in educational provision, there is an ever-increasing number of ways of studying.

❏ **Case Study: Clem**
*Clem had gone into teaching for positive reasons, but saw it as only a temporary stage in his career. After a while, he began to see it as too easy an option and not a 'proper' job. He also wanted more autonomy, grew tired of being 'governed by bells' and was afraid of getting stuck and being too old to turn to other options. He resigned without any other work arranged.*

*What happened next, he readily admits, was unsystematic and carried out with little commitment. He applied for lots of jobs in business administration and met with no success. He began to get depressed and his self-confidence waned. A careers counselling session helped him to recognize the common threads running through his previous experience, to reflect on how he had made previous career decisions and provided him with a framework for deciding on his next career step. He subsequently invested a lot more time in researching his options and identifying the people he could talk to in order to make his career decision. In the end, he decided to take a post-graduate course in careers guidance and, once started, experienced a tremendous sense of relief that he had at last 'found something'. The course had not only trained him for a particular kind of work, but had also developed his self-confidence and self-belief, and, what is more, given him an occupational identity.*

## WORK RELATED TRAINING

It is important to distinguish between initial pre-entry training for a particular occupation and training within the context of one's work.

This latter form of development activity is very often concerned with skill acquisition and technical knowledge and can take place 'on-the-job' and 'off-the-job' at courses, workshops and other training events. Both have their merits. On balance, it is probably more difficult to gain access to training outside the immediate workplace without investing your own time and money, but the rewards can be greater. You will be more likely to have your training validated by a professional body, or a particular educational institution, and will almost certainly extend your network of work contracts and increase your awareness of opportunities elsewhere in the workplace.

❏ **Case Study: Hitesh**
*Before working as an information officer, Hitesh had experience of desktop publishing – skills which were important in his current job. It was this experience which gave him exemption from the first year of a part-time course in DTP and graphic arts. By doing the course, he hoped to gain accreditation for his previous experience, develop his own skills and creativity in a field in which he was interested, and gain a qualification which would make him more marketable. The course, a mixture of lectures in typography and practicals in DTP with a strong creative element, was not easy for someone with a natural science degree, but Hitesh managed to hold his own with the designers on the course. In retrospect, there were positive outcomes. He gained a definite sense of personal achievement and, in particular, felt more confident about his creativity, and one component of the course stimulated his interest above all others – photography, a subject Hitesh wants to develop for his own interest. There were also implications for his present job – commissioning graphic design and print work had become much easier with his newly-acquired knowledge and at the same time he had become more critical of his own design work. The qualification, of course, recognized and validated his earlier experience.*

CONTINUING PROFESSIONAL DEVELOPMENT

Those already established in a particular career may have no thought of changing, but simply want to gain greater professional recognition among their peers or keep up to date with changes in professional practice. Most professional bodies will encourage their members to make a commitment to continuing professional development in order to maintain levels of competence or to progress to the next level of accreditation. The precise form of this development can vary. Many refresher courses on, say, current legislation and its implications may be covered by short courses, but programmes which offer a qualification will invariably be longer and often involve distance learning or independent learning, as the following example illustrates.

### ❑ Case Study: Nina

*As a teacher with responsibility for special needs provision in her primary school, Nina had become particularly interested in child behaviour and now in mid-career, she wanted a fresh challenge, the chance to develop her intellectual capacity. The Certificate and Diploma programmes in 'Applied Professional Studies' at the local university gave her an ideal opportunity to develop her understanding. Apart from a taught course on child development, the programme consisted largely of independent study based on the testing and observation of children in the classroom. As well as studying child behaviour she also researched methods of raising children's self-esteem and worked with a particular child with organizational problems.*

*Although it was some years since her initial training, and she had difficulty meeting deadlines for assignments as well as coping with family demands, it was a positive experience. She had gained a sense of achievement and improved her own understanding and ability to cope with special needs children. Also, the programme had helped in advising other teachers in the school. There were, therefore, obvious benefits to her job performance. And while the qualification would prove no advantage to her career in her own school (it was too small), Nina recognized that it would be advantageous if she moved to a larger organization. What is more, the diploma carried with it an opportunity for rapid progression to a Master's degree.*

## SECONDMENTS, PLACEMENTS AND INTERNSHIPS

The notion of the 'stage' or work experience placement is common throughout France and Germany. Those completing education and training frequently have a number of paid or unpaid placements to build up a portfolio of relevant skills and experience. They are available in business and management, social services and education, as well as other employment sectors. The notion of a six-week or three-month work placement is far less common in this country, except in the case of higher education students on sandwich courses. Generally, employing organizations have been unwilling to take on those in mid-career for a short-term placement. Work experience has, in the main, been seen as an important and valuable adjunct to the educational process and therefore mainly available to students at all levels.

In the United States, the term 'internship' is used to describe a similar process, but frequently internships are available to graduates, diplomates, and those who have already completed their education. The advantages of the stage or internship are obvious:

- Participants gain a clearer picture of the work in which they are interested.

- They use skills and knowledge already gained.

- The professionals they work alongside often provide mentoring relationships, offering information and guidance on job availability and long-term career prospects.

For those in early or mid-career, the opportunities for placements and secondments are less obvious, with the exception, perhaps, of the teaching profession. Here, exchanges between teachers of different countries, teacher secondments to business organizations often orchestrated by school/industry link organizations, are reasonably common. However, secondments and volunteer placements are becoming increasingly common, and given the ever-changing flexibility in work styles and employment contracts it seems likely that more professionals will be able to take advantage of them. They can certainly provide a powerful development experience, as the following case study shows:

## ❑ Case Study: David
*David had spent ten years with the same employer and desperately wanted a career move. His work role was, however, fairly specialized and with a young family he wanted to stay in the same geographical area. He decided that one possibility was to change to a job involving research and, in order to test out this idea, he organized a paid six-month placement with a locally-based but nationally-known research organization. He negotiated a paid sabbatical from his present employer on the understanding that his 'host' employer would finance the salary of his full-time replacement (albeit at a lower level) – an arrangement which worked out well for all concerned.*

*The sabbatical proved to be an eye-opener. David realized that his knowledge and skills were immediately transferable to a research setting, in particular those concerned with interviewing and report writing. He had gone from a low prestige role in a large organization to a higher prestige job in a small organization. In six months, he had completed and written-up one research study and contributed to the field work of an even larger project. His self-esteem and self-confidence improved dramatically. Suddenly, new career avenues seemed to open up where none had existed before. His colleagues firmly expected him not to return to his old job. At the end of his sabbatical he did return, however, but the experience proved invaluable in confirming his own value in the job market, in extending his network of professional contacts and seeing what it was like to work in a more dynamic environment.*

These case studies illustrate some of the many forms of development experience. In your own situation what might be the most interesting or rewarding form of development activity?

Paying attention to your personal development, at whatever level, can have a range of positive outcomes. It might provide a greater sense of fulfilment and life satisfaction. You may find that you cope more effectively in your present work, develop existing or new skills, generate new ideas or increase your network of personal contacts. More broadly, it can also increase your own effectiveness as a learner, improving your self-confidence and ability to be proactive on your own behalf. For those concerned with continuing professional development (CPD) there will be the opportunity to keep up to date with new areas of professional practice or technical knowledge, while at the same time adding to the level of their professional accreditation.

An increasing commitment to your own personal development can also bring about hoped-for change in your career. By demonstrating new-found workplace skills and competencies by having your experience accredited or by increasing your level of qualification, you are demonstrating your potential both to your current and also to future employers.

For those considering fresh career ideas, or those making initial choices, one particular point of tension arises over the question of 'Is it possible?' We may have ideas about what we would like to do but doubt our confidence to do it, or assume that the competition for what we want is so great that our chances of gaining access are slim. We may therefore reluctantly decide to set our sights on 'realistic' goals, on what we know is achievable, rather than work for an ideal job or career. If we are already in work we may even content ourselves with the notion that staying in our present job appears to be a reasonably viable option, and that rather than expend energy on the search for alternative options and making applications, we make the best of our present situation.

## *YOUR PERSONAL DEVELOPMENT AGENDA*

*EXERCISE 5.1*

What commitment are you going to make to your own personal development? What are your immediate development needs? The following exercise may help you clarify your ideas and indicate what you might achieve:

What recent development activity have you engaged in?


What would you now like to achieve? – to develop particular skills; a professional qualification; meet other work needs?


What difference will it make to you and your career?


What information do you need about what development options are available? How will you go about putting your plans into practice?


How will you know when you have achieved your goal? What evidence will you have of your involvement?


There is no one particular way of resolving this issue. In the end, our propensity to try to implement our preferred goal will depend on the amount of motivation and impetus we have. Very often, however, our feelings of inertia are conditioned by our self-efficacy, the level of confidence we have in ourselves to make life changes successfully, and our knowledge of what is likely to be expected of us in new work situations. It is for this reason that various forms of personal development provide such a powerful impetus for change. New-found confidence in our ability enables us to effect change, but also to cope with new challenges and work situations.

# Chapter Six

# Strategies for Choice, Change and Maintenance

*Among highly adaptive individuals, men and women who are truly
alive in, and responsive to, their times, there is virtual nostalgia for
the future. Not an uncritical acceptance of all the potential horrors of
tomorrow, not a blind belief in change for its own sake, but an over-
powering curiosity, a drive to know what will happen next.*

Alvin Toffler, *Future Shock*

Previous chapters have illustrated the process of career planning –
of how to shape your career thinking and determine the next move
in your career development. But in both maintaining your career
and in carrying out change, there are various tactics, skills even,
which you may need to rehearse. The present chapter is therefore a
*tour d'horizon* of the steps you can take to implement career choices
and changes successfully. It is by no means exhaustive but offers a
range of methods you can adopt as a matter of routine.

For too long we have assumed that 'careers' will look after
themselves and that the coping processes associated with career
development come naturally and need little in the way of
enhancement or development. That indifference was perhaps
understandable in a more stable employment market, based on full
employment. Now, however, things have changed and will
continue to change more rapidly than before. We work in a less
certain and more competitive job market. We need, therefore, to
invest more time in maintaining and shaping our careers if we are
to gain some satisfaction and self-esteem from the work we do. We
need to take charge of our own careers. Your starting point will, of
course, depend on your present situation.

For those leaving education with little work experience, the idea
of 'choosing' a career is often problematic for a host of reasons.

There is often immense perceived pressure to make the 'right' decision. Many graduates, in particular, feel that having invested in higher education, they have to do the 'right' thing when they complete their degree. The range of options may seem bewildering, and at the same time there may be apparently contradictory messages about what options are realistically available. There is often also a fear of commitment to one particular job or employer. A very real temptation is to put off the idea of having to make a decision, to procrastinate, by taking time out to travel the world.

For those in mid-career, there are different concerns. Career decisions have implications for partners and immediate family. They are not necessarily taken on the basis of individual needs and wants. There are, too, other concerns about the option of retraining, both in terms of the costs involved and the length of time it might take, bearing in mind the age bias incipient in the job market. Making a large financial investment to educate yourself further may well need to be taken in the light of your expected financial gains and the difficulties of re-entering the job market at a later stage in your career. The more complex the decision and the greater the range of factors involved, the more imponderable career decisions become.

It is not surprising, therefore, that an expression frequently used by people facing career choices and decisions is 'feeling stuck'. It is a common experience for those making initial career choices. It sums up succinctly the sense of immobility experienced by many who are unhappy in their present situation, but feel unable to make any significant change to their lives. In some cases this is because it is difficult to identify what is going wrong – to pinpoint the exact cause of their dissatisfaction. In others, it is because of the barriers that appear to be in the way of change.

As one potential career changer put it, 'I have so little time to think things through, given the demands of my present job. My kind of work is quite specialized and there are few, if any, jobs advertised locally. I need to know who will employ me. At the same time, I'm restricted geographically. My partner is a block on my career and being a parent puts a constraint on what is possible. Money is always a problem and there is no career progression where I work already'.

The issues raised here will probably sound familiar and resonate with many in the workplace.

There are a range of factors which can inhibit our career development. The most frequently cited is lack of self-confidence.

Those returning to work after a career break, or the long-term unemployed, often give way to self-limiting or self-defeating beliefs. They frequently underestimate what they are capable of achieving and suffer from a negative self-image. In short, they doubt their own ability. Fear of rejection and fear of change can also be contributory factors. Putting yourself forward for a job or

## OVERCOMING BLOCKS ON CAREER DEVELOPMENT

### EXERCISE 6.1

The aim of this exercise is to list the blocks you may be facing in your career development and identify ways of overcoming them; an analysis of problems and possible solutions. Simply list the things that are holding you back and then, perhaps with a friend or partner, list the ways of moving forward. There may, of course, be more than one way of overcoming the obstacles you appear to face. It assumes that you have some kind of direction or goal in mind, however tentative.

| **Blocks to your career development** | **Possible solutions** |
|---|---|
| e.g. I have an idea of what I want to do for a living but don't know who to talk to. | e.g. Phone professional or trade associations to make contact with a local member to learn more about the idea. |
| e.g. My skills seem out of date. | e.g. Take a refresher course to confirm and improve my skills. |

When you review your list of 'possible solutions', it is quite likely that some of the items will be concerned with your personal development. Others are likely to be activities concerned with career change and job search – the practical tasks that you need to carry out to test out your career ideas and put them into practice. What follows is a summary of the things you can do to bring about career change and the activities you can engage in to maintain your career effectively.

promotion can also expose you to the full rigours of selection and assessment processes, and repeated failure in the selection process will inevitably lead to a reluctance to face yet another rejection.

By far the most common barrier in career choice is lack of information. We simply do not know about the options available. On the one hand, we are not familiar with trends in the job market or where jobs might occur, but also we have only a vague impression of what these jobs might involve. There is a risk that we simply think in job stereotypes rather than try to understand in detail what each kind of work might involve. Very often we may exaggerate the demands of particular jobs or employers, further reinforcing our sense of 'can't do' rather than 'can do'. The sheer number of options is often a potential source of confusion. As one career changer put it, 'There were times when I wished I lived in a Communist state, so that someone would tell me what to do with my life'.

There is therefore something of a paradox. For some people, career choices are concerned with narrowing the range of options to focus on one or two types of work. For others, the aim is to discover at least one option for which they are qualified and in which they might find success. One response to the barriers that seem to block our career path is to turn potential problems into a personal learning objective which can be acted upon. Exercise 6.1 may help.

## USING GUIDANCE SERVICES

Many people, quite naturally, turn for help when making career choices and changes, firstly to family and friends and then to guidance professionals. But what can you expect to gain from seeing a careers counsellor or other guidance professional? How can you make maximum use of the services on offer?

To a large extent, this will depend on the way those engaged in careers counselling choose to work around the particular range of services they offer. What follows is a review of the range of methods used by guidance practitioners, with guidelines on how you might benefit from them. On the one hand, there are private, fee charging agencies involved with outplacement and career development counselling, whose work with clients may involve detailed personality and aptitude assessment, followed by counselling interviews and a written report. On the other, careers services for those in education and training will offer a range of guidance services which include the use of computer-assisted guidance systems, access to occupational information and advisory interviews. The range of professional practice in this area varies widely but *au fond* there are a number of basic processes which characterize all guidance activities. According to Kidd (1988), both careers and educational guidance can have one or more of seven different functions:

- informing – providing factual information on options available

- advising – on appropriate courses of action

- counselling – helping clients articulate their needs

- assessment – making judgements about choice suitability

- enabling – coaching clients in dealing with agencies

- advocating – working on a client's and provider's behalf

- feeding back – gathering information for training providers on unmet training and development needs.

Notions of 'advocacy' and 'feeding back' characterize the work of educational guidance specialists; the other functions typify careers guidance practice. The balance of the guidance services available will reflect the resources and overall philosophy of the guidance provider. Most guidance for those in education involves the use of information centres on a self-help basis, access to a careers adviser for an advisory/counselling interview and, if necessary, placement help. Adult guidance centres, where they exist, are most likely to offer short 'assessment' interviews, in conjunction with the use of computer-assisted guidance systems. The following summary is designed to show what you might expect from guidance providers.

## ACCESS TO INFORMATION

A major concern of career planners is to know what is available, and to different degrees guidance providers will offer access to occupational information about different work areas, details of education and training opportunities and potential employers. Typically, the emphasis will be on published materials already in the public domain. The 'insider' view of occupations and organizations will, therefore, be lacking, but there are ways of overcoming this shortfall, as described in the section 'Researching your options'.

Most careers guidance centres on the process of counselling, of a one-to-one helping encounter between the client and the guidance professional. This is the area in which you will find the widest variety of professional practice, with some advisers basing their guidance on the results of psychometric tests and others relying on the use of the counselling interview.

If you want to know what to expect from such an interview, it will help you considerably if before you consult a guidance professional, you ask the question 'How do you work with clients?' The reply will help you to assess how they approach their work and clarify your own expectations. In the main, however, you should be offered at least the opportunity to discuss your career concerns in confidence, as part of a structured interview which centres on you, the client, and your needs. Indeed, according to Kidd *et al.* (1993), most career advisers would tend towards an approach which is client-centred, non-directive and designed to help 'empower' those seeking help.

## COMPUTER-ASSISTED CAREER GUIDANCE SYSTEMS

A wide range of computer-assisted guidance systems now exist to help users in the career planning process. They are, it has to be acknowledged, only as good as the systems designers and bear the hallmark of the original developer. They offer a starting point, but one which may not appear relevant to the needs of the user. They can, however, fulfil an important function. Broadly, there are four different kinds of software, each with a different level of complexity:

- information databases providing details of occupational information and education and training opportunities
- matching systems offering a simple match between individual self-assessment and occupational titles
- tutorial systems, which coach the user in curriculum vitae or job application writing and production
- learning systems designed to teach users processes such as career planning and the concepts associated with it, for example, skills identification and self-assessment.

In a number of cases they can be used without reference to a guidance professional, but in general their availability is mediated by careers guidance staff and for good reason – the results of CACGS usage have the potential to confuse as well as enlighten!

One problem in their use is the unrealistic expectations of users. All too often, clients expect to be presented with the ideal job or career option rather than acknowledge that the aims of 'matching' systems are to illustrate a range of options rather than predict the job for which the user will be ideally suited. Their lack of availability, particular to those already in work is another factor inhibiting their use and a proper understanding of their potential. With these caveats, however, CACG systems can be invaluable to the user in:

- finding out the latest information about courses of further education and training

- researching the entry requirements for different occupations

- reviewing personal skills and interests

- obtaining 'option lists' and ideas for further research.

## CAREER WORKSHOPS

Although not widely available, career workshops offer an effective way for the participant to determine career objectives. Pioneered particularly by women's groups, they can also be offered by employers, by professional associations and, of course, by guidance services in higher education. They usually involve 12 to 15 participants, all with similar concerns, in a process of career review and action planning, using many of the self-appraisal methods common to other forms of guidance activity. Participants are usually invited to review their previous experience and their present career stage in order to define career future goals. The process resembles the career planning cycle described in Chapter 2, and is summarized in Figure 6.1 below which is based on the Kolb learning cycle and described by Harrison *et al.* (1992).

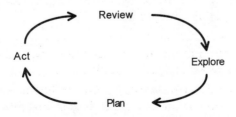

*Figure 6.1:* Based on the Kolb learning cycle.

The advantages of career workshops are several. Firstly, they enable participants to share perceptions and problems in a relatively 'safe' environment. Secondly, they provide a day of activity devoted exclusively to 'career', an unbroken period of time given to self-appraisal and reflection. Finally, however, they offer the opportunity for new learning about self and career options, as well as changed perceptions and assumptions about possibilities for personal and career development. Indeed, it is the 'fresh insight' which many participants claim to receive which facilitates personal change. Although there is little research evidence in the UK as to the outcomes of career workshops, it is clear that they have considerable potential in enabling participants to identify changes they would like to make in their careers and their lives generally, and prompt them into implementing these changes.

## PSYCHOMETRIC ASSESSMENT AND PROFILING

A number of guidance agencies, particularly those offering private careers guidance services, as well as outplacement consultancies, offer psychometric profiling for individual clients. This can involve the use of personality measures and interest inventories as well as aptitude tests to build up a profile of the abilities and personality characteristics on which to make recommendations about particular kinds of career direction for the participant. The assessment is therefore concerned exclusively with guidance. You can receive feedback which will help with decisions about your general career direction.

It is important, however, to make use of properly trained and accredited guidance professionals, because so much rests on the proper interpretation of test results. Psychometric assessment has the power to undermine self-confidence as much as to increase it, and it is vital that clients are encouraged to use the results of assessment constructively for their own personal and career development. What can you expect to gain? Naturally, given all that has been described about change in the workplace, it would be unrealistic to expect to be put on the ideal career path for life, as a result of the helping processes available. And yet, commonly, clients of guidance services do have unrealistic expectations of what can be achieved and occasionally raise questions such as 'Now that we've been talking for 15 minutes, what kind of job do you think I'm suited for?' They expect to be matched to a suitable career with the minimum of effort. More realistic expectations might include having feedback on the design of a CV or an 'expert' view of the job market.

So what, realistically, can you expect to gain from using guidance services? Almost certainly you should be able to gain a different perspective, a revised view of the options available to you and, in particular, awareness of the range of information sources available to you. Secondly, you can receive reassurance about your present situation and the plans you may be considering. This should, in turn, increase your self-confidence. In her review of a number of research studies which focus on the outcomes of guidance, Carroll (1989) points to the potential of guidance in helping individuals to clarify their career plans and hence make their job search more effective. In addition, you may well gain greater self-knowledge and understanding as a result of guidance activities, since, as we have seen, nearly all the methods currently used pay particular attention to self-appraisal and life review. You may also be ready to start putting your plans into action.

## PROACTIVE WORK AND JOB SEARCH

'I look at the local paper but the right job doesn't seem to appear.' For most people the main sources of information about job vacancies are the 'situations vacant' columns of local and national newspapers followed, perhaps, by recruitment agencies and job centres. And if the kind of vacancies which interest them don't appear, then they assume the jobs don't exist. It is very much a reactive approach to job search.

An alternative strategy put forward by adherents of 'creative' job search, involves, according to one American writer, 'finding the person who has the power to employ you'. This favours an entirely different approach to work search based on detailed research, speculative applications and networking. It is particularly appropriate in times of recession or high unemployment. What can it involve? Quite simply, it involves putting yourself forward to prospective employers and letting them know you are available for work. Advocates of this approach argue that work search is not simply a question of who you know, but rather 'who knows you'. They point to the fact that many vacancies are not advertised but filled by internal appointments, and, if they are about to be advertised, employers can save themselves the costs of advertising if they have before them the details of suitable applicants. There are other arguments in favour too. On the one hand, employers may have short-term work to offer – research projects, training, consultancy, but may be reluctant to advertise for freelancers, and so a carefully-targeted CV may be the most appropriate way of eliciting well-paid work as opposed to permanent employment. On the other hand, employers may not have recognized their staffing needs fully, and a well-made speculative application might just convince them that they need another member of staff to handle their increasing workload.

Proactive work search can, in theory it seems, meet with success, but it calls for a considerable amount of preparation and effort on the part of job seekers. In particular, creative approaches require you to:

- be clear about your career aims; potential employers can only respond positively if they have a good idea of the work you are looking for;

- research potential employers in terms of their location, organizational size and structure, and likely human resource needs;

- produce very convincing written applications using a curriculum vitae which is well honed and professionally presented;

- make an effective argument for the way your qualifications and experience can assist in the employer's activities, highlighting in particular your skills, personal qualities and previous relevant knowledge and experience;

- target particular individuals in an organization so that your application avoids routine rejection, but receives careful consideration by the departmental manager or other individual who has the power to appoint staff.

It is difficult to predict what kind of response this approach will bring. At the very least you should get an acknowledgement, perhaps a promise to keep your details on file or even information about other employers who have a vacancy. Ideally, however, you may be offered a formal or informal interview and from that point on, the decision will be concerned with how you would 'fit' with the other people in the organization. If all else fails, you will have at least made potential employers aware that you are available, and they may be able to let you know of immediate job opportunities in other organizations. In effect, you have the chance to tap their professional network for information about possible opportunities.

A word of caution may, however, be necessary. Many large organizations will not be able to make instant recruitment decisions on the basis of a simple CV, but will expect applicants to go through a protracted selection process (see below). While you may, therefore, be able to attract the attention of a senior manager at Unilever or an under-secretary at the Foreign Office, you will still need to go through formal selection procedures. But this is not to deny the value of the activity, particularly for yourself. One possible outcome of the creative approach to job search will be the increased confidence you may gain from seeming to be in control of the situation rather than being dependent on recruitment advertising for providing you with possible options. Your self-esteem may well increase as you start taking action on your own behalf.

## PROMOTING YOURSELF EFFECTIVELY

Whether you are looking for freelance work, preparing a job application or applying for placement or 'stage', there are a number of ways of improving your chance of success. A study by Atkinson *et al.* (1994) highlighted eight characteristics of successful job search based on earlier research findings. These were:

- self-confidence and commitment

- realistic occupational focus

- breadth of approach to job search

- balanced use of employers' vacancy channels

- professional presentation to prospective employers

- persistence and continuity of job search

- filing and recording of possible vacancies

- periodic review of plans.

In completing the career planning exercise in Chapter 3, you may well have gained a clearer sense of career direction and therefore be able to target your applications more effectively.

If you have made use of guidance services, you may well have increased your self-confidence to enable you to make a positive application. There follows a summary of how you might bring the other factors into play in your work search in order to ensure success in your applications. One key factor will be your ability to learn from the selection process in order to improve your chance of achieving what you want. If you fail with a particular application, try to analyse why this came about, perhaps by asking the recruiters for some feedback about your application. If the jobs in which you are interested do not appear in the vacancy listings, try to discover the reasons for this.

While the selection process is obviously designed chiefly to help employers make recruitment decisions about who to recruit, it can also offer the candidate – the job seeker – an opportunity for personal learning. For those unsure of their career decision, it offers the chance to have their career ideas confirmed, or not, as the case may be. If, even in the face of rejection, you are still committed to your career plan, it suggests that the kind of work you are looking for may still be consistent with your overall aims. At the same time, the more rigorous selection processes involving assessment centres may also provide you with a revised view of your own abilities and values, because of the degree of personal assessment that is involved.

Yet again, by participating in the selection process you are also developing your self-presentation and communication skills – in being interviewed, in taking part in discussions or in making a presentation. While it may appear daunting, the job selection process can provide both increased self-insight and awareness and offer the chance of rehearsing and improving your skills in coping with similar situations.

There are numerous books offering hints and tips on effective job search, on coping with interviews and designing an effective curriculum vitae. It is not the aim of this chapter to repeat in detail the convential wisdom concerning applications and interviews. What is provided, however, is an overview of the main tactics you can employ to meet the criteria for effective job search highlighted earlier.

## RESEARCHING YOUR OPTIONS

Having access to up-to-date information is a key requirement for deciding on career options, as well as for making effective applications. On the one hand, we need information to make decisions and to choose between different options, and on the other, the better researched your applications, the more likely it is that they will be successful. The information we require may be of various kinds, some of which are readily available and accessible, whereas others may be difficult to come by.

For those wanting to change direction in mid-career there are particular problems in gaining access to information which is relevant to their needs. Most published occupational information is written for school and college leavers and usually concentrates on entry qualifications and initial training routes. Information of this kind seldom allows for the idea of career conversion at a later stage, or takes into account relevant work experience or training in different but related fields. At the same time, those making initial choices meet problems of a different kind. Occupational information concentrates largely on conventional employment and work styles rather than the more esoteric. It also provides basic information about entry qualifications but frequently ignores the 'insider view' of what it is actually like to do a particular kind of work. Data on employment trends are extremely difficult to access, because the research organizations publishing such material charge, rightly, a high price for the results of their work. In short, published careers information, while valuable, has its limitations. As a result, therefore, we need to use a range of sources to gain the information we need, and adopt alternative methods of enquiry.

Several research studies have pointed to the value of using first-hand information sources to access what Hayes (1971) refers to as the 'psychosocial' aspects of the work, reflecting the 'full reality of occupations'. Factors such as lifestyle, organizational culture and social relationships become increasingly important to people once they are established in their jobs.

A study by Boreham and Arthur (1993) yields some interesting findings about the way that different groups use and value information sources. For the adults in the study it was clear that the world of work (as opposed to media, family and friends, and school) was seen to have the greatest use in providing information for occupational decision making. For the unemployed group, in particular, 'speaking to someone in the job' was adjudged to have the highest value. The findings lend considerable support to the idea of informational interviewing in making and implementing career choices and decisions.

The technique of informational interviewing is both simple and effective. It requires you, the job seeker or career changer, to interview someone who is involved in the particular work you would yourself like to do. By asking questions about the job content, the competencies required and the likely rewards, you can build up a detailed picture of the work and then decide whether it will match your interests.

## UNDERSTANDING EMPLOYER NEEDS

There are numerous books on effective job search which describe the job seeking skills you need in order to find the kind of job you are looking for. In particular, they give advice on how to design a CV and how to interview well; they are designed to help you cope with selection processes. There are two other aspects of job search which you will need to bear in mind even before you put your job-seeking skills into practice. Both require background research into topics which are not easily researchable. Both have an important contribution to the success of your job search, but are not always taken into account by those looking for work. They concern recruitment practices and selection criteria:

- What are the typical recruitment 'norms' in the particular part of the job market in which you are interested?

- How do particular employers carry out their selection process? What criteria do they use for selecting applicants?

Finding answers to both questions is vital to successful job search.

## MAKING SENSE OF RECRUITMENT PATTERNS

Employers have different motives for recruiting staff. Some larger employers may even employ a mix of different approaches. For example, typical graduate entry programmes might include one of the following:

- a fast-track development scheme leading to posts in senior management, perhaps lasting several years, often with a managed sequence of postings

- a programme of professional training lasting three years, involving formal study in preparation for professional examinations

- a direct entry to particular jobs within the organization, with a training and development programme to suit individual needs

- short- or medium-term training programmes which can last anything from six months to three years, combining general management training for particular business functions.

The different needs of employers will determine how they recruit. For instance, graduate recruiters with over 50 vacancies offering a training programme are likely to plan their recruitment well in advance on the basis of their human resource needs. Targets will be set a year ahead of graduate starting dates. In their recruitment process they will require all applications to be received by a given deadline, perhaps in January each year and an extended selection process then takes place to find final-year students to start work in the following September after graduation. This process is the norm for most of the large private sector graduate recruiters. By contrast, local authorities, small businesses and consultancies are more likely to recruit to fill specific vacancies and will advertise their vacancies at any time of the year, looking for staff to start as soon as possible.

The average job seeker is therefore faced with a range of different recruitment practices, but many of these are sector-specific. Retailers, on the whole, will behave like other retailers, advertising agencies like other advertising agencies and accountancy firms like other accountants. Some employers will need to rely heavily on media recruitment advertising, others will receive so many unsolicited applications they will have no need to advertise for staff. The job seeker's task is to find out which rules apply among the employers they are targeting and for the particular jobs they are seeking.

## IDENTIFYING SELECTION CRITERIA

The more difficult task is to find out about the selection processes used by employers and the criteria they will be using. For example, you might want to question how much weight they attach to results of selection tests, or what style of interviewing employers usually adopt, or what proportion of applicants they call for interview after their pre-selection process.

Generally, the selection process is characterized by a number of stages, each consequent upon the other, but the precise pattern will vary. The process may include:

- pre-selection of written applications;

- first or preliminary interviews;

- a second-stage selection process which may include psychometric tests and 'group' assessment exercises or further interviews.

If you pass the first hurdle and are offered an interview, it is reasonably easy to find out what kind of selection process might be in store for you, simply by phoning the personnel department or the member of staff responsible for selection. In fact most employers make these arrangements perfectly clear to those applicants they are about to interview.

Understandably, perhaps, employers are usually reluctant to make public the precise criteria used in the selection process, but it is possible to gain a fair impression of the kind of person they are trying to recruit by carefully reading the job particulars or recruitment brochure. Again, it is the job seeker's task to glean as much as they can from any printed material available or by talking to people already employed in the organization.

Typically, a large graduate employer, for example, will be looking for a range of personal qualities and attributes in addition to particular qualifications or academic achievement. These might include qualities such as motivation and drive, skills in communication and working with people, awareness or knowledge of their particular industry as well as evidence of career commitment. Often these criteria are clearly signalled in the design and content of application forms. Graduates, however, are often surprised that employers are more interested in finding out what they can *do* as opposed to what they *know*. Indeed some employers attach considerable weight to personal skills. As one UK graduate recruitment manager put it, 'An applicant with strong personal skills but weak academically is more likely to be interviewed than a candidate who is strong academically, but shows poor personal skills'. This may be a minority view, but it reveals the importance given to personal skills by many employing organizations.

Small employers are likely to have different concerns. They will probably not be able to make a big commitment to training, but look for people who can make an immediate and effective contribution. One of their main criteria will be the amount of relevant previous experience offered by candidates rather than any longer-term, and as yet undemonstrated, potential.

## MAKING A MATCH

When researching career options, one very useful tactic is to send for details of advertised job vacancies. The advertisement often conveys the minimum of useful data, but the additional information made available to applicants can reveal considerably more about the organization and the jobs in question. The information you gain from this approach can be useful in helping you to see the kinds of opening available, but also to help you to match your own profile of knowledge, skills and interests with the jobs in question. If you decide to go a step further and make an application, the following three-stage procedure will help you make a convincing application:

*TEASE OUT THE JOB DESCRIPTION*
Most employers will be able to send an outline job description of the vacancy they have on offer. If it lacks any useful information, you can simply phone for more precise details to identify the key aspects of the job.

*DRAW UP A PERSON SPECIFICATION*
Personnel specialists may have already determined the kind of criteria they will be using to select candidates. They will have drawn up a specification for the ideal candidate in terms of experience, qualifications and skills. If they provide this for you, you have a head start; if not, you will need to analyse the job description to profile the kind of candidate the employer will want to interview.

## MAKING A MATCH

### EXERCISE 6.2

*When you have gathered as much information as you can about a particular vacancy, try to analyse precisely what you have to offer.*

| Job description | Person specification | What you can offer |
|---|---|---|
| List each of the job activities, e.g. managing a team, carrying out research | For each activity, identify the particular skills that may be required | List the attributes you can bring to the job in question |

*IDENTIFY YOUR OWN PROFILE*
Finally, you can list the range of positive points from your own experience which you can put into your written application. The prompt sheet will help you complete the processes already outlined above.

When you have finished your analysis, you can identify possible gaps in your experience or skill profile. It will be particularly useful at this stage if you can find someone else to look at your results. Have you missed a key point? Have you exaggerated the need for particular experience? Have you omitted to highlight skills you have and which are directly transferable to the job in question? A second opinion, particularly from a guidance professional, will almost certainly help. Finally, be sure not to eliminate yourself because there are one or two gaps in your profile. A potential employer may be more interested in your particular attributes than any apparent 'deficits' in your work experience.

# A STRATEGY FOR CAREER MAINTENANCE

If you are happy to stay in your present job, rather than look for a career or job change, there are a range of steps you can take to maintain your motivation and possibly tailor your work more closely to your particular interests. We tend to focus our attention on 'careers' at times of crisis, when faced with a life transition or because of growing unhappiness with our present job. Typically, graduates leaving university, women returning to work after a career break, recently redundant managers and professionals, will all want to review their career prospects when faced with personal change of the kind described. When work is going smoothly, when we are relatively happy with our lot, we tend to expect that our career will look after itself. There seems little point in reviewing a career that may be developing slowly but satisfactorily in a direction which is consistent with our needs and career anchors.

Circumstances change, however. A new manager, a new company structure, a revised job description can all prompt a career review. Indeed, it is possible to identify a cyclical process which we may go through in a particular job. Initial motivation and interest gives way to indifference as we become more familiar with the job content and the work appears more routine. Kilburg (1991) calls this phenomenon the 'doom loop'. When we start a particular job, we are keen to learn and perform well. The longer we spend in the job, the more likely it is that we become bored to the point of dissatisfaction both with the job and ourselves. The diagram below illustrates the trajectory of the doom loop over time.

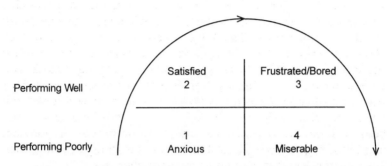

*Figure 6.2:* The doom loop.

According to Kilburg, there is a major risk to our self-esteem if we fail to acknowledge that this process is taking place. People who see their career as a permanent life sentence are very likely to find themselves trapped in box 3 and there are major risks to their self-esteem if they find themselves slipping into box 4, resulting in 'bitter self-disempowerment' and an inability to make change for the future. Our task, therefore, is to recognize this process should it occur, and rather than accept it as an irreversible trend, take action to sustain our work interest and self-esteem.

Indeed, there is a range of activities we can engage in to ensure that our career continues to develop in a positive way, rather than remaining unattended and on a downward trajectory.

## MAINTAINING A PERSONAL NETWORK

As we saw in the freelance case studies earlier, networking is an essential ingredient both in securing work and also in gaining support from fellow freelancers working in the same area of business. It is becoming commonplace now, however, to see net-working as an essential activity for all those at work, offering, as it does, a range of potential benefits. The most commonly cited benefit relates to job search. People hear about job vacancies from relatives or 'on the grapevine'. Others are simply approached on the basis of personal recommendation. Whatever the precise mechanism, it is clear that many people owe their jobs to well-meaning friends and acquaintances who have simply passed on information about a vacancy and urged them to make an application. Having an extended network of personal contacts can, it is claimed, make you better informed about the opportunities for career development. There are, however, other reasons for developing your personal contacts in and outside the workplace, which are perhaps less instrumental but equally rewarding.

If you are feeling undervalued in your present work, if you suspect that your line manager is likely to block your career advancement, or sense that you have skills and expertise to offer which are not being put to good use, you can certainly benefit by talking to other staff in your organization, perhaps outside your own department. They may be able to provide a form of counselling support, offer suggestions about alterations you can make to your work situation and encourage you to make the changes required. Gaining support from members of staff in your organization is obviously one form of networking. Their knowledge of the organization's culture and politics may be particularly valuable.

Friends outside work and immediate family can provide the same kind of personal support, but so too can fellow professionals working for other employers. Indeed, the kind of networking offered by professional associations has a particular advantage – it may enable you to bring into play the same career maintenance strategies and tactics that fellow professionals have found successful elsewhere.

One specific form of networking involves the adoption of a mentor figure. Many of us are aware of those people who have helped us to progress and develop. They may be family, friends, teachers, people in the workplace, or fellow professionals working in other organizations. Usually older, they have acted as both a guide and role model. When it occurs naturally and spontaneously, this form of mentoring can have considerable benefits for both mentor and protégé. From the mentor's point of view, it is gratifying to help someone benefit from your own experience. From the protégé's perspective, there are a wide range of tangible gains from a relationship which offers support and encouragement over a period of time.

Given the potential of the mentoring process, there is increasing interest in the notion of formally assigned mentors, particularly for those undergoing training programmes in the workplace, in which younger entrants are matched with older and experienced staff. The functions of mentoring are outlined in the following:

| *Career Functions* | *Psychosocial Functions* |
|---|---|
| Sponsorship | Role modelling |
| Exposure and visibility | Acceptance and confirmation |
| Coaching | Counselling |
| Protection | Friendship |

(Source: Greenhaus and Callanan, 1994)

At a basic level, mentors can offer information about the organization, its structure and culture and about job opportunities within it. They can offer feedback on how well the protégé is performing in the light of the expectations of line managers. As the mentor/protégé relationship develops and greater trust is established, the mentor can increasingly take on the role of counsellor and confidant in resolving problems and difficulties or clarifying the protégé's career aspirations and suggesting a suitable strategy for achieving them. This may sound very fine in theory, but does it work in practice? An increasing body of research evidence suggests that mentoring can offer a variety of work- and career-related outcomes which include greater career mobility, work satisfaction and recognition. For this reason, there is considerable interest in introducing mentoring programmes for those from ethnic minorities and for women managers in avoiding the 'glass ceiling' effect.

There are, however, doubts as to whether formal mentoring schemes can offer the range of benefits which arise from informal mentoring relationships and about how far one mentor/protégé relationship is sufficient to make a significant difference in work performance and career advancement. Perhaps the mentoring process is most usefully seen to operate across a range of workplace relationships. According to Thomas and Kram (1988), 'Individuals should be encouraged to develop and nurture a constellation of relationships that reflects their career and psychosocial needs at successive career stages'.

DEMONSTRATING YOUR EFFECTIVENESS

Most of us would take for granted the idea that we need to perform effectively in our work in order to gain the approbation of workmates or line managers. After all, the way our work is perceived may have a direct bearing on pay and promotion.

Those on precarious short-term contracts will understand the importance of delivering work to a particular standard in order to secure a renewed contract. Established freelancers will also appreciate the need to gain repeat work and, as importantly, be introduced to other clients on the basis of personal recommendation. Most of us will therefore be keen to demonstrate competence in our current work, for reasons of self-esteem if not for those already mentioned.

In part, of course, this can be achieved by relatively simple methods: by delivering work on time, taking care over presentation, by adhering to professional standards. There are, however, other tactics which enable us to enhance our perceived effectiveness. One is to maintain your visibilty with those around you, especially line managers and work colleagues. By providing evidence of your achievements – evaluating the success of your work, in contributing to the completion of new projects or becoming involved in the activies of professional associations, you can create a positive impression. Demonstrating success in this way is particularly important for those who naturally prefer a background rather than a high-profile role, but who none the less work effectively and put considerable energy into their work.

## WIDENING YOUR PORTFOLIO

'Growing in the job' is for many of us the only way to maintain motivation, and keep our interest alive, if the opportunities for career progression and advancement are no longer available. There are numerous ways of widening the range of your experience so that you not only increase your own sense of worth, but become more valuable to your present employer and of greater interest to potential employers. You can, for instance, become expert in a particular field and increase your technical or job-related knowledge. You can broaden the range of your experience, so that you offer a variety of skills and become flexibly adept. You might engage in development activities which extend your personal effectiveness in managing your own work as well as that of those around you. In short, there are numerous ways of extending your portfolio of skills and experience.

For people in full-time jobs, whose every minute is accounted for, this may sound a somewhat fanciful notion, but if you have any discretionary element in your work or have opportunities for personal development, you may like to consider ways in which you can deliberately set out to increase the range of your experience. It is not uncommon, for example, for university lecturers to work as external examiners for other university departments, or for scientists or engineers to devote time to their professional associations, or for social workers, for example, to contribute to training programmes and courses of professional development.

In all these instances, the individuals concerned are allocating some of their time to activity which feeds back into their everyday work and enhances their satisfaction from work. If you work as a part-time professional, the opportunities to engage in consultancy, freelance and other forms of work, naturally increase. This experience can not only 'feed' your part-time employment by allowing you to develop particular expertise which is valued by your colleagues, but also meets needs which are not being met in your 'permanent' part-time job. It may also boost your self-confidence because freelance work inevitably involves an element of choice. You can, therefore, choose the work you enjoy most and hence maintain a measure of personal success. And if your freelance work happens to be with a prestigious organization, so much the better for your own status in the eyes of colleagues.

As you will have seen from the previous chapter, keeping a commitment to your development can ensure the currency of your personal skills and increase your awareness of opportunities for career development and enhancement. Inevitably, there may come a time when you feel you have simply outgrown your current role and no amount of job enrichment will sustain your motivation. You know that to rekindle your interest in work, or even avoid further burn-out and stress, you need to give yourself a fresh start. It is at this point that the career planning processes outlined in earlier chapters will come into play as you embark on a change in your career and a review of the options for further career development.

# Chapter Seven

# *Your Career Competencies*

*There is in every organism, including man, an underlying flow of
movement toward constructive fulfilment of its inherent possibilities,
a natural tendency toward growth.*

Carl Rogers, On Becoming a Person

There are a number of problems in writing a book on the subject of
career choice, change and development. One concerns the word
'career.' For many people 'career' is still associated with the idea of
progression to higher paid jobs, of movement up the management
hierarchy, rather than the broad view of our life's work, which
includes both personal and career development and a variety of life
roles.

Secondly, there is the view that 'careers' are the province only of
the professional or semi-professional, and that shop-floor workers
have 'jobs', not careers. According to this perspective, the notion of
career is bound up with class, status and occupational level. It is an
appropriate description, therefore, of the behaviour of some but not
all individuals in the workplace.

It may also be argued that uncertainty surrounding the
workplace, high levels of unemployment and uneven distribution
of work further invalidate the notion of 'career', because of the lack
of continuity in paid employment.

One of the messages of *Assessing Your Career* is that the idea of
'career' continues to undergo a reformulation over time, and will
increasingly need to reflect a growing variety of work roles and
statuses. 'Career' remains, for most of us, however, an appropriate
and convenient label for descriptions of the work we do in
whatever context, as well as our attendant lifestyles.

There is also the question of personal autonomy. Those taking an optimistic view of the change and uncertainty in the job market will argue that we can adapt to the new employment scenario and that, by being flexible in our approach, we can cope with the shifting demands of employers and the highs and lows of the business cycle. According to this view, individuals have a degree of choice in deciding what kind of work to do and they make choices, autonomously, on the basis of the match between their own aspirations, qualifications and skills, and the opportunities available. And although we may not be able to meet all our career needs in one single step, it's possible progressively to find work which is satisfying and fulfilling.

A counter voice, however, will argue that it is government economic policy and economic performance generally which determine the number and range of opportunities available to us and, furthermore, that the changes that have taken place in the job market work largely to employees' disadvantage. According to this view, the 'opportunity structure' defines and creates work opportunities and is more of a determinant of our career development than our own autonomy and ability. Advocates of this more pessimistic view will argue that we need greater realism in our career thinking and must take the options that are available rather than entertain unattainable goals. One implication, therefore, may be that we need both to recognize the constraints that may be operating on our life chances, but at the same time hold on to the hope and aspirations we have for our future careers.

Furthermore, there is a question of neutrality. Is it possible to provide a guide for career changers which is value-free? How far are the changes in the workplace to be welcomed and seen in a positive light and how far are they to be resisted? For example, there's no reason to suppose that people want greater flexibility and uncertainty in their working lives. Indeed there is every reason to believe, as research has shown, that people need security in employment in order to ensure regular income and provide a basis for other life decisions. The 'portfolio' workstyle portrayed in earlier chapters may therefore represent a less than ideal bargain for individual workers. Its formulation may have served as a smoke-screen to hide the reduced commitment employers are making to their employees.

Yet again it is clear that in a contract work culture, the responsibility for career development and management rests almost entirely on the individual. Flatter organizations, unable to offer career progression in the conventional way, will increasingly find ways of devolving this responsibility to their employees, whether they are 'core' or 'contract.' Freelancers, perhaps working at the edge of several different organizations, will obviously be responsible for their own futures.

In order to cope effectively with this new employment scenario, however, we are increasingly having to develop our self-management skills when facing career issues. Few people have been taught skills in managing their careers; we acquire them largely as a result of experience. As we pass through different career stages, work in different organizations, we gradually gain greater insight into how to handle our working lives. We come to understand the processes involved and the skills and competencies which are required.

A summary of the major competencies is outlined in Figure 7.1 below. Four competencies in particular:

- optimizing your situation

- engaging in personal development

- using career planning skills

- balancing work and non-work

underpin the processes of career choice, change, maintenance and adjustment. What follows is an analysis of these competencies in terms of the skills and behaviours involved in each of them.

*Figure 7.1:* Competencies for career development.

## COMPETENCY 1:
## OPTIMIZING YOUR SITUATION

One of the characteristics of career development is the propensity of individuals to improve their lot, to find work which is more interesting, better paid or more in accord with their personal values. They strive continuously for greater fulfilment, satisfaction and reward. Being able to make career moves and changes which work in your favour will obviously bring into play your career review and planning competency and require you to keep sight of what motivates and interests you.

However, you may also need to adopt other strategic career behaviours. In its most obvious sense, this might suggest being highly goal-orientated in your behaviour, knowing what you want in the long term and deciding how to achieve it. As we saw in Chapter 6 there are various ways that those at work can achieve this – by networking, gaining recognition for their achievements, working with staff who are seen as high performers, or generally projecting a positive self-image. For those who are 'core' workers in their organizations, these are the 'smart moves' which get you noticed and help you progress up whatever organizational ladder exists – the route to conventional career success.

But there is a broader, more creative approach to career strategy which is important for 'portfolio' workers as well as for those in a single permanent job. This involves being able to anticipate changes in the workplace and manage your responses accordingly. If you sense a change in the economic environment which will have a negative effect on your work, or you know that your main employer is in merger talks with a competitor, you can prepare contingency plans. Equally, if you know that government legislation or technical change is likely to create opportunities, you can make a conscious attempt to keep career options open rather than close them. To have 'a finger on the pulse' of change of this kind can help you predict its outcome and the impact it might have on the demand for your services.

By knowing how to cope with change and manage life transitions – from employee to freelancer; from career break to part-time employment – you can increase your sense of purpose. You can put yourself in control of events rather than being a victim of change. This involves more than simply being opportunistic; it implies taking a considered approach designed to meet your career needs. There is, however, one further dimension to having a strategic approach to career: that of having a short- or medium-term view of how you want your career to develop. One American writer has called this phenomenon 'having a career capstone'. Simply stated this means having a broadly defined goal to work towards, rather than a planned sequence of career moves.

Those who have graduated from university with little work experience will recognize the need to gain experience, skills and further qualifications before they achieve their career goal. Becoming a qualified social worker, operating as a freelance journalist or television programme producer, or working abroad as an accountant – are all examples of medium-term career goals, achievable some years after graduation. In many cases the jobs they eventually find might be entirely new. One recent follow-up study of university graduates revealed that one in three respondents were in jobs that had not previously existed – proof positive of the extent of change in the workplace.

The same principle applies equally to those in later career stages. You may already have developed a particular specialism in your current work and perhaps be able to foresee a new work role which does not yet exist, or a new product which is not currently available. By assembling the right mix of experience and a particular range of knowledge and skills you may be preparing yourself, consciously or unconsciously, for a new area of work which as yet may not even have a title. This ability to envision future opportunities is another example of strategic career behaviour; of being able to create and make your own chances. It's a form of well-considered opportunism.

## COMPETENCY 2: CAREER PLANNING – PLAYING TO YOUR STRENGTHS

It should be clear from the changes taking place in employing organizations that we need to ensure our adaptability in the job market. We need to adjust to change and cope effectively with the consequences. You will already have seen the career planning model outlined in Chapter 2 and have realized that *Assessing Your Career* is built around the career planning cycle of personal review, option searching, and taking action to put your ideas into practice. In a work environment characterized by rapid change we need to review our career progress more frequently, and the career planning process enables us to do this.

You may be working and midway through your twenties when you feel that the work you are doing is not going well. You experience dissatisfaction and feel the need to cast around for other options. You might be facing redundancy in your late forties and be contemplating a complete career change. Or you could be returning to work after a career break, anxious to maintain your employability. Whatever your exact situation, you can use the career planning cycle to review, plan and make changes in your working life. You need to use the same set of skills:

- defining your needs and interests (self-appraisal)
- researching options for change or progression
- pulling together the results of your appraisal and research
- taking action to put your ideas into effect
- communicating effectively with those who can employ you.

However, the process is not one to be undertaken only for the purposes of change. It can also be used when making minor adjustments to your work in terms of its content, or the time you invest in it. In short, career planning can be used for career maintenance, for gaining a progressively better fit between your needs and the work you do. It will encourage you to:

- review to what extent your work is satisfying your needs and interests
- prepare for job opportunities that might arise – new jobs that have not yet been created
- recognize what you need to do to move on in your career
- learn from mentors, partners and colleagues
- define and set goals for the future.

There are therefore several contrasting activities. On the one hand you can see career planning as the ability to compete effectively in the job market, to produce convincing applications and to make sure that you perform well at selection interviews. On the other hand, there is the more reflective and research-like activity of understanding how employers recruit, and what kind of employment trends are taking place. Most importantly, however, there is the ability to stand back and reflect on your own life experience, and to work towards your future goals.

Yet again, career planning competency is as important for 'portfolio' workers as it is for those who are 'permanently' employed. The research skills involved are as relevant to the freelancer who is looking for potential clients as it is for the job seeker. The presentation skills involved in CV preparation and interview performance are the same skills that freelancers require when tendering for research or consultancy contracts. The self-review skills are equally valuable. The skills involved in career planning are therefore transferable to any work setting, and any style of working.

Finally, and most important, the very process of using and enhancing your career planning skills should help in maintaining your self-belief and self-confidence. It is quite clear that there is a large affective component in making and implementing career changes which will make you feel happier or more satisfied with your work. You will need to feel confident about your ability to make change and, when faced with rejection, you will need to keep alive your motivation and commitment.

Working through the career planning process and developing your skills in this domain should help you to do this.

## COMPETENCY 3:
## BALANCING WORK AND NON-WORK

We all have different ideas about the amount of our lives we want to invest in work. Junior hospital doctors may be reconciled to spending most of their waking time on call. Freelance editors and designers may have more discretion about their use of time and can decide how many days a week they are prepared to work, depending on the volume of work at any one time.

For most of us, however, there is little discretion. We are tied to particular hours of work and are often obliged to work additional hours. Indeed the term 'overtime' seems to have lost its original meaning in today's labour market, one in which we are expected to work longer hours for no extra reward. Perhaps the 'portfolio' future will enable us to have more discretion over when and how we work and allow us to negotiate with our employers for greater flexibility. It is a big 'perhaps'.

In many cases it will be our values which determine how much time we invest in work. In Schein's view (1978), those of us with career anchors such as 'pure challenge' or 'entrepreneurship' may well be prepared to spend more time at work than those who are concerned with 'lifestyle integration' – valuing flexibility such as the ability to take sabbaticals, work flexible hours and so on. Quite simply, some of us are prepared to work longer hours than others. Whatever our priorities, however, we are all faced with the issue of balancing the often competing demands of home and work, of reconciling our commitment to personal relationships and family with the demands of an employer or client. Furthermore, the balance between the different areas of our lives is never static; it is influenced by life events. For example, if your partner is made redundant and you are working part time, there will be an urgent need to increase your working hours in order to cope financially. When experiencing work strain or 'burnout', there will be a similar immediate need to review your work commitment. By responding rapidly to changed personal circumstances there is always the chance that we can create a work style and working arrangements which fit our particular needs, rather than making do with a less favourable situation.

Typically, our motivation at work varies with our life stage. Those approaching retirement, for example, very often want to 'disengage' slowly from the workplace by lowering their commitment, reducing their responsibilities or shortening their working hours. Parents keen to give time to child rearing can also be faced with similar concerns. Equally, we need to be aware that any change in values may prompt a review of the amount of time we want to invest in work. Very often the career changer is driven by a desire to make major lifestyle changes, and often this involves a reduction rather than an increase in time spent at work, to reduce the balance in favour of leisure or 'development' time. It is precisely because the relationship between work and non-work is never static, but ever-changing, that managing the interface between the two is a competency we need to acquire. There is also every indication that the 'problem' becomes more intricate in a 'portfolio' workstyle. Conventional employment – going out to work at an employer's premises – enables us to separate home life and work life. It provides us with a different environment in which to operate. Imagine, by contrast, the freelance homeworker sitting at the home workstation – one minute answering a school circular, then completing a request from a client, and then organizing childcare. The world of home and work is one; there is no separation between the two. Suddenly, setting work priorities and effective time-management become crucial when you determine your own pace of work rather than have the pace determined by those around you. Being able to balance work and non-work becomes even more important rather than less.

## COMPETENCY 4:
## ENGAGING IN PERSONAL DEVELOPMENT

If there is a new psychological contract in employment, it is largely this: employers no longer able to offer lifelong continuity of employment, let alone career progression, are increasingly offering opportunities for employees to further their personal development. The rationale is quite simply that a continuing investment in your personal development is likely both to refresh your skills and maintain your motivation. Being stuck at a particular career level will not be seen as evidence of your lack of ability or commitment; rather it will simply reflect the organization's structure. Your development needs will still have to be addressed. But what are the consequences for the individuals concerned? How will we need to respond?

Firstly, we need to be effective learners. When faced with continuing personal and professional development we have to be aware of our feelings about learning, and how our previous experience may have influenced our attitudes. We may have to overcome 'blocks' to further learning such as lack of self-confidence or previous experience of failure. We also need to be aware of our preferred learning style. Is team working preferable to independent study? Is our approach to learning essentially active or reflective? The range of learning styles that people habitually adopt is the focus for a number of self-rating questionnaires (Honey, 1992). Naturally, having a range of personal study skills is important in this regard, but so is an understanding of how we learn best, and in what circumstances.

Secondly, we have to be able to identify our development needs and how they can be met. A new job or project will be the stimulus for a development review, so that we can set goals for our immediate training needs. Equally, the process of reviewing development is vital in maintaining our careers. We need to be able to recognize our susceptibility to stress and identify its causes, to monitor our health and the ways we are coping, or not, as the case may be. We need to acknowledge feelings of demotivation and at the same time recognize those elements in our work which offer us most satisfaction and be aware of ways in which our work could be enhanced or enlarged to give us a greater feeling of reward. We need to recognize that underemployment can be as much a cause of work strain as overwork. It is only after the process of reviewing our needs that we can begin to see how they might be met.

Finally, we may have to negotiate access to the opportunities on offer. For many forms of development activity – in-house training, project work, mentoring – there will be few barriers to participation; indeed, it will actively be encouraged. In some circumstances, however, access will be more difficult and negotiating access can take two forms.

For those in employment, training and development needs are often discovered by the appraisal process. A key ability is to negotiate with your manager to do the things you want to do. Inevitably, in this situation, it is the employer who largely defines any training needs because their main concern is your work performance. Your overall well-being and sense of fulfilment comes second. It is therefore often quite difficult to gain financial support for non-vocational training or courses which relate primarily to your own personal interests, although some large companies have begun to fund programmes of this kind. Sometimes a degree of compromise can be reached, but this will only happen if you are going to define assertively your own development needs and negotiate with your manager in order to have your ideas taken seriously.

For all of us, the same negotiating skills will be useful in gaining credit for our previous experience and training when applying to programmes of further study or when attempting to meet the qualification requirements for professional membership. Very often, there is an element of discretion which can be used by admission tutors in allowing access to courses to potential students with 'non-standard' entry qualifications, and in giving potential students educational credits and possible exemption from particular course modules. Very often it will be up to the individual to demonstrate and provide evidence of their prior learning. Once again, the ability to negotiate effectively will assist your cause.

## YOUR OWN FUTURE

The descriptions of the four competencies for career development should give you an idea of the kinds of behaviour we need to adopt to be able to cope effectively with workplace change, both now and in the future. It is not intended as a prescription – more a way of highlighting the key issues which we are all facing. In learning how to cope effectively we should be better able to manage our careers in a way that meets our needs and interests, and to assert our own ideas.

So, in summary, what of your plans for the future? How do you envisage your own career developing? The questionnaires in Chapter 3 will have provided you with your own personal profile and your appraisal of skills and interests may have already given you career ideas that you want to research further. Now, however, you may like the chance to describe any change you would like to make in your life as a whole, as well as to describe your plans for work and career.

The Personal Review Questionnaire which follows is designed to help you clarify your short-term and longer-term goals for personal and career development. In one sense it can be seen as an agreement to be made with yourself about future life changes. Your replies to the questionnaire should provide a positive agenda for action, and you should feel free to describe everything you would like to achieve.

What you write in your 'career success' questionnaire should give you some insight into what you might want to accomplish in future – the kind of life and workstyle change you envisage, the skills you need to develop, as well as your values and career anchors. You might, for example, explain your need for promotion in terms of the higher salary it would bring, or the release it offers from your present boredom or the chance for you to tackle new and demanding challenges. Either way, you will gain an insight into your motivation for change and development.

Alternatively you may want to anticipate life events and transitions that will affect your career; having children and a career break or a change in the time you spend at work; taking early retirement with the intention of working as a freelance consultant; or coping with an impending redundancy. Whatever the case, being able to stand back from your immediate situation will help you arrive at solutions to your career 'problems' and, perhaps, prompt ideas for your future development. Even if what you hope will happen appears at first to be fanciful and unrealistic, you will at least have given yourself the freedom to think positively and creatively about your future – you will have defined career success for yourself.

## ── *PERSONAL REVIEW QUESTIONNAIRE* ──

### *EXERCISE 7.1*

### **WHAT DOES CAREER SUCCESS MEAN TO YOU?**

1. Thinking about your life and work, what would you like to be doing in a year's time? What change, if any, would you like to make to your situation? Try to describe in some detail the immediate plans you might have for your life and work.

2. In three or four years' time where might you be? What kind of future would you like to see for yourself? Here you can describe your longer-term goals and take into account any further investment in education and training. You can point to particular skills or experience you might want to gain, or anticipate life stage changes.

3. What will you need to do to arrive at the point you want to reach? When you have listed the action points you need to take, try to assess what implications there might be for your personal development, then see if there are particular issues you need to think about that have been covered by *Assessing Your Career*.

4. Finally, reflecting on your experience to date, what would you still like to accomplish? Are there hopes you have been cherishing that have not so far been realized? Things you would still like to achieve? How might these ideas be brought to fruition?

# REFERENCES

Atkinson, J. (1994). *Jobsearch: Modelling Behaviour and Improving Practice,* Report No. 260. Sussex: Institute for Employment Studies.

Bannister, D. (1982). 'Knowledge of Self' in Holdsworth, R. *Psychology for Careers Counselling.* Leicester: BPS Books (British Psychological Society) (now out of print).

Berg, I. (1970). *Education and Jobs: The Great Training Robbery.* London: Penguin.

Boreham, N. C. and Arthur, T. A. A. (1993). *Information Requirements in Occupational Decision Making.* Sheffield: Dept. for Education and Employment.

Carroll, P. (1989). *The Potential of Guidance for Making Jobsearch More Effective.* Sheffield: Dept. for Education and Employment.

Daniel, W. W. (1987). *Workplace Industrial Relations and Technical Change.* London: Frances Pinter.

Dyer, W. G. (1983). *Contemporary Issues in Management and Organizational Development.* Reading, Mass.: Addison Wesley.

Fagenson, E. A. (1989). 'The mentor advantage: perceived career/job experiences of protégés versus non protégés.' *Journal of Organisational Behaviour 10,* pp 309–320.

Fletcher, C. and Williams, R. (1985). *Performance Appraisal and Career Development.* London: Hutchinson.

Frederikson, R. H. (1982). *Career Information.* Englewood Cliffs, N.J.: Prentice-Hall.

Freeman, C. and Soete, L. (1994). *Work for All or Mass Unemployment: Computerised Technical Change into the 21st Century.* London: Pinter.

Fritchie, R. (1990). 'Biography work'. *The International Journal of Career Management,* 2, No.3.

Ginzberg, E. (1972). 'Toward a theory of occupational choice: a restatement.' *Vocational Guidance Quarterly,* March, 171–172.

Greenhaus, J. H. and Callanan, G. A. (1994). *Career Management.* Orlando: Harcourt Brace.

Haddon, L. and Silverstone, R. (1995). *Teleworking in the 1990s – A View from the Home.* University of Sussex: Science Policy Research Unit.

Handy, C. (1984). *The Future of Work.* Oxford: Blackwell.

Handy, C. (1985). *Understanding Organisations*. London: Penguin.

Handy, C. (1993). *The Age of Unreason*. London: Arrow Books.

Harrison, R. *et al.* (1992). *A Portfolio Approach to Personal and Career Development*. Milton Keynes: Open University.

Hayes, J. (1971). *Occupational Perceptions and Occupational Information*. Bromsgrove Institute for Careers Guidance.

Holland, J. (1966). *The Psychology of Vocational Choice*. Waltham, Mass.: Blaisdell.

Honey, P. (1992). *Manual of Learning Styles*. Maidenhead: Honey.

Huws, U. (1994). 'Teleworking in Britain.' *Employment Gazette*, *February*, 51–5. London: Dept. for Education and Employment.

Inkson, K. and Coe, T. (1993). *Are Career Ladders Disappearing?* Corby: Institute of Management.

Jackson, C. (1990). *Careers Counselling in Organisations*, Report No. 198. Sussex: Institute for Employment Studies.

Jackson, C. (1993). 'Mentoring: choices for individuals and organisations.' *The International Journal of Career Management 5*, 10–16.

Kidd, J. M. (1988). *Assessment in Action*. Leicester: NIACE.

Kidd, J. M. *et al.* (1993). *Working Models of Careers Guidance: The Interview*. London: Dept. of Organisational Psychology, Birkbeck College/NICEC.

Kilburg, R. (1991). *How to Manage Your Career in Psychology*. Washington, D.C.: American Psychological Association.

Kram, K. E. (1986). 'Mentoring in the workplace' in Hall, D. T. and Associates (Eds) *Career Development in Organisations*. San Francisco: Jossey-Bass.

Levinson, D. J. (1978). *The Seasons of a Man's Life*. New York: Ballantine Books.

Lewis, J. and McLaverty, C. (1991). 'Facing up to the needs of the older manager.' *Personnel Management*, 32–5.

Maslow, A. H. (1987). *Motivation and Personality*, 3rd edn, London: Harper and Row.

Mayo, C. (1992). *Managing Careers: Strategies for Organisations*. London: IPD.

Meager, N. *et al.* (1994). *Self Employment and the Distribution of Income, Report No. 276*. Sussex: Institute for Employment Studies.

Newman, K. S. (1993). *Declining Fortunes – The Withering of the American Dream*. New York: Harper Collins.

Schein, E. (1978). *Career Dynamics*. Mass.: Addison-Wesley.

Stonier, T. (1983). *The Wealth of Information*. London: Methuen.

Super, D.E. (1981). 'Approaches to occupational choice and career' in Watts, A. G. *et al.*, *Career Development in Britain*. Cambridge: CRAC/Hobsons.

Thomas, D. A. and Kram, K. E. (1988). 'Promoting Career-Enhancing Relationships in Organizations: The Role of the Human Resource Professional' in London, M. and Mone, M. E. (Eds), *Career Growth and Human Resource Strategies*. Westport, CT: Quorum Books.

Watts, A. G. (1993). 'Refocussing on common ground: future directions' in *Building a Learning Culture*. Cambridge: CRAC/Hobsons.

# Index
compiled by Frances Coogan